George Laurence Gomme

The Literature of Local Institutions

George Laurence Gomme

The Literature of Local Institutions

ISBN/EAN: 9783337205614

Printed in Europe, USA, Canada, Australia, Japan

Cover: Foto ©ninafisch / pixelio.de

More available books at **www.hansebooks.com**

THE LITERATURE

OF

LOCAL INSTITUTIONS

BY

GEO. LAURENCE GOMME, F.S.A.

LONDON

ELLIOT STOCK, 62 PATERNOSTER ROW

1886

PREFACE.

The interest of this little work to book-lovers will, I hope, be twofold. At a time when local muniments are being examined and edited, and at last preserved from the wholesale destruction of past years; and when the Bill in the present session of Parliament for the enfranchisement of Copyholds provides by one of its clauses that the whole of the most important class of historical documents in this kingdom, namely, the manor rolls, shall be delivered up to the world of letters, it is time for the book-lover to take stock of what has been already accomplished towards printing these and other records.

A further result of this little work is that the book-lover is able to place at the disposal of thinking men some idea of the extent of the literature of local institutions; and, by indicating how important that literature is, to urge that it should not be neglected now that current *thought is so much occupied with the question of reform in local government.*

Local institutions have been the subject of study with me for many years, and I had hoped ere this to have published a long-projected volume dealing with their early history in this country; but my many avocations, official and private, have prevented this cherished idea ever being completed. The materials collected for this undertaking, however, are of great value; and the books which have from time to time been consulted, form a branch of literature which is now being fully recognised as perhaps the only source of information on the social manners and customs of the people in the past. Nothing had ever been done to bring this literature together until, in 1882, in the BIBLIO-GRAPHER, *I gave some instalments of the subject. The interest excited by these papers encouraged me to proceed in collecting and describing books on the literature of local institutions, and the present volume is the result of these labours.*

It is useless to hope that my collection of titles

is absolutely complete—so many books of this class have been privately printed, or else printed for purely local purposes, and have hence not found their way into the general market. The British Museum is notoriously deficient in this branch of literature. I have in nearly all cases consulted and used each work referred to. To many of the titles I have given special bibliographical information. Where such information is not given, it is generally because no practical good would come of such information. In some instances I am indebted to kind friends for references to out-of-the-way works, and I must particularly mention, at the risk of being invidious, Mr. J. Newman, Mr. W. Macmath, Mr. R. B. Prosser, Miss Lucy Toulmin Smith, and the late Professor Stanley Jevons and Mr. Cornelius Walford. My visits to the libraries of the two last-mentioned scholars and book-lovers will not be easily forgotten; and it was this subject which first took me thither.

Of the faults, both of commission and omission, in this book, I trust a kindly view may be taken; and for any information helping me to fill up gaps, or correct errors, I shall be deeply thankful. Even as I go to the press, too late for insertion in their proper places, two very interesting additions may be made to the literature of local institutions, namely, a translation of Gneist's great work, which is mentioned on page *13*, and Miss Toulmin Smith's edition of Lady Caroline Kerrison's Commonplace Book of the *15th* century.

Barnes, S.W.

THE LITERATURE OF LOCAL INSTITUTIONS.

INTRODUCTION.

ENGLISHMEN of the nineteenth century are just as active in the "making of England" as their ancestors were in the early period to which the title of Mr. Green's famous book refers. And it must ever be so : the means and process differ as the ages differ ; but it must be a question of *making* England until that period arrives when the downward progress commences. Closely connected with this continuity of development are the powers and privileges of local government. When the Saxon conquerors of Britain carved out the boundaries of our modern shires by their ethnic settlements; when they settled down in their several village communities, they were solving in their own fashion — the only one then possible—the future of local government in England.   Shire- and hundred- and township-government went on developing under native Saxon rule, until the progress of political events declared the necessity for strong central government. The up-growth of Saxon kingship and sovereignty was the result of this inevitable and inexorable necessity ; but Saxon kingship and sovereignty, even aided by the Roman influences still extant, could not answer all needs.   The time came when the exigencies of the constantly pressing events demanded the surrender of much of the powers of local government to the central government.   And the Norman conquest marks very strongly the age of this surrender.

I do not think it is too much to affirm that the central authority has been built up by taking to itself, one by one, or bit by bit, all the powers which originally belonged to local authorities.   The process has been a long one, and very insidious ; and it has been greatly aided by the uniform persistence of one of the most remarkable of legal fictions. All English, and indeed all European, jurists have ever had before them the splendid legal system of Rome ; the lawyer's education begins with the study of Roman law, and he has never had any professional occasion to consult the barbarian codes which mark the true beginnings of English law. All legal history, in point of fact, lay outside his knowledge or requirements, and hence all legal theory has been developed from the finished system of a civilised code of law. When, therefore, the analytical jurist came to consider the momentous question of the origin of law, he could only see before him the central sovereign power which lent its sanction to the carrying out of the behests of the law, and he very easily identified law with the coercive force of the sovereign power. The terminology of this definition is, of course, borrowed from the modern authority of John Austin, but the maxim it represents is to be found throughout the legal authorities of the middle ages, and has lain at the

root of all legislation. It was the grand
fiction which the Norman lawyers worked
upon, and to which Norman power owes
more than half its enormous sway. When
William the Norman came to these shores
he found strong local centres of power,
already tending to decay, it is true, but
still strong. He did not sweep away these
local centres, but he gave them charters
and taught them to believe that the
sovereign was the source of all their legal
authority. The peace of the land became
the "king's peace". The law became
"king's law". Justice became "king's
justice". The courts became "king's
courts", and the judges who sat there became the servants of the crown in theory,
if not in fact. All the local jurisdictions
leaned towards the central powers. Lords
of manors, with the old rights of "sac and
soc", surrendered their lands and had them
regranted, or they forfeited them and thus
allowed them to become the actual regrant
of the sovereign to faithful adherents and
followers.

This, stated shortly, is the process which has been going on in England since the Norman conquest, and it has witnessed the total surrender of all legal rights to the central authority, the final stage being marked, perhaps, by tne transfer in 1877 of local prisons to the authority of the Central Home Department.

It is not a little curious to the student, knowing this to have been the true course of events in the history of local institutions, to observe how ministers and political reformers, of all sides and all shades of opinion, appear before the public to advocate the conferring by Parliament of the blessings of local government upon the English people. To read some of the speeches of the foremost politicians in England, it would seem as if, from their own sense of what was required for the government of a country, they had wisely decided that, at last, local institutions should be founded. And yet what a mockery such a proposition is. Nearly all that is now being urged as appertaining to the privileges of a newly created system of local government—local option, land allotments, county boards, and other important subjects—has always belonged to the old local institutions, and has never been taken away from them by any legal or constitutional enactment. The insidious legal doctrines already spoken of have, however, done the work of the ruthless destroyer most effectually; and when the Municipal Reform Act of 1835 was passed amid acclamation as a distinctly popular measure, people did not know that its very first clause was, perhaps, the only parliamentary enactment which cut at the root of the very municipal institutions which later on were to be advocated so forcibly. This clause is as follows :

"'Whereas divers Bodies Corporate at sundry Times have been constituted within the Cities, Towns and Boroughs of England and Wales, to the intent that the same might for ever be and remain well and quietly governed ; and it is expedient that the Charters by which the said Bodies Corporate are constituted should be altered in the manner hereinafter mentioned' ; be it therefore enacted by the King's most Excellent Majesty, by and with the advice and consent of the Lords, Spiritual and Temporal, and Commons, in this present Parliament assembled, and by the Authority of the same, That so much of all Laws, Statutes and Usages, and so much of all Royal and other Charters, Grants and Letters Patent now in force relating to the several Boroughs named in the Schedules (A) and (B) to this Act annexed, or to the Inhabitants thereof, or to the several Bodies or reputed Bodies Corporate named in the said Schedules, or any of them, as are inconsistent with or contrary to the Provisions of this Act, shall be and the same are hereby repealed and annulled."

If this enactment does not actually abrogate all old municipal rights, and that I suppose is open to legal argument upon the question as to what is inconsistent with the act, it does so virtually, because it has taught municipalities to look to Parliament for all their powers. And yet, if they were to look beyond their charters and their Acts of Parliament, they would find that of old such rights as local option, and much more than we now include under that term, had a place in their rights and privileges, as may be seen from the records of

such towns as Dundee,[1] Sandwich,[2] Nottingham,[3] Chesterfield,[4] and even London
herself ; they would find that at one time
in our history municipal boroughs appeared as land-owning communities, where
every freeman had his right to a share in
municipal lands, where the community
could resume the ownership of the land
upon the death of a present owner, and
where the community had almost absolute
power over a great deal of the real property
in its area;[5] they would find, in short, in
the history of local institutions, that most
of the powers now proposed to be conferred
as a blessing at the hands of this or that
political party, already exist, but have been
lying dormant and unused as portions of a
social system which has become obsolete.

If, therefore, the history of local institu-

[1] *Cf.* Maxwell's *History of Old Dundee.*
[2] *Cf.* Boys's *History of Sandwich.*
[3] *Nottingham Borough Records.*
[4] *Chesterfield Borough Records* and Mr. Yeatman's
Introduction.
[5] Some of the details of this I have set out in
Archæologia, vol. xlvi, pp. 403-422; in *Antiquary*, vol.
ix, pp. 157-162.

tions point to such interesting facts as these
—facts which may guide modern politics in
its course—is it well to ignore it so persis-
tently ? or at all events is it not a mere
matter of ordinary wisdom that we should
make ourselves acquainted with it before
trying our 'prentice hand upon a machinery
so delicate as national institutions ? In
answer to these very obvious questions
arising only from this necessarily very short
survey of the subject, the following notes
have been put together. They are practically the working materials by which I
have studied the subject for many years past
—the skeleton, which I hope one day may
be clothed in such a manner as to bring
before us a true picture of the past, but which
in the meantime may help to serve the
purpose of those who take an intelligent
view of the object and aims of future legislation. In addition to this primary object,
there is the feeling that the notice of these
books, old and new, may form a not unin-
teresting fragment of a book-lover's library.
All of them have had human hands at work

upon them, most of them have occupied
the attention of some of our best thinkers,
many of them are the product of good
sound scholars and bookmen, who turned
their attention to such a concrete subject
because they knew, as we ought to know,
that to think properly and wisely of the
future we ought to know of the past. And
there is much, very much, of human interest in this subject. Municipal and town
records tell of men as well as of institutions;
and occasionally these men who took active
parts in the government of their native
places are of such universal interest as John
Shakespeare (the father of our poet), who
successively filled the posts of ale-taster,
assessor, burgess, constable, chamberlain,
alderman, and high sheriff at Stratford-
upon-Avon. Many of the municipal officers
of London became the founders of great
and distinguished county families — an
interesting fact, which has scarcely received
the attention it deserves.[1] And when we

---

[1] Pennant touches upon this subject in his *Tour through London* ; and Defoe, in his *Tour through England*, draws special attention to it.

add to these phases of our subject that the
church formed the centre of local life,
that the holidays were holy days, that
all festivals were church festivals, that
the overseers and churchwardens are one of
the bodies corporate who administer parish
matters, and that the registers, account
books, etc., of these bodies are our chief and
sometimes only means of obtaining information on the most important and interesting phases of family and social history in
the past, it will be admitted that the subject has far wider interest than at first sight
would appear. Before the days of "Regis-
trars-General," parish registers existed, and
everyone knows how universally these have
been recognised as documents of the greatest
value. Almost all the secular usefulness of
the church has now departed, but it is still
a question whether Englishmen will allow
that institution to drop out of the sphere
of local government without a struggle to
make it again an instrument for good in the
daily life of the people. By spiritualising it
overmuch we have lost its grand secular in-

fluences for good ; but the English village, or town, or city, is still crowned by the church edifice to make it complete in picturesque outline; and if we knew all about old English village life, old English local government, we should yet make it the centre and head of local life in the future.

I must guard myself against the supposition that the following pages are intended to give an exhaustive account of the literature of local institutions. They aim only at pointing out how extensive that literature is; what are the best guides to learn the history of any particular section of the subject; and to urge, in the strongest possible terms, that it is not well to cast all this literature on one side as useless for future guidance.

I.—LOCAL INSTITUTIONS GENERALLY.

SOME important books have appeared upon the local institutions of England taken as a whole, and so important has the subject been to foreign students, that it is a curious fact that the best account is written by a foreigner, and remains still in its foreign language, viz.: Gneist's *Geschichte und heutige Gestalt der englischen Communalverfassung.* Professor Kovolefsky, of Moscow, has been investigating the subject recently, and he expressed his great surprise to me that so little attention was paid to it by Englishmen. The result of his labours may, it is hoped, soon see the light, and there may be some chance, perhaps, of putting it into an English dress. But by far the most interesting studies are those which have lately been engaging the attention of American students. The Johns Hopkins University has instituted a series of studies on historical and political science, under the able editorship of Mr. Herbert B. Adams. In this series have been investigated the local institutions of Virginia and Maryland ; dealing with the land system, the hundred, the parish, the county, and the town. From these two very important books are to be gained some most instructive lessons as to the application of the principles of the local institutions of England in the seventeenth century to an entirely new country and settlement ; and it is greatly to be hoped that the university authorities, more alive to the requirements of the age than the authorities in England, will pursue these studies, until they have exhausted the rich and varied evidence which must be forthcoming.

The following are the principal works on the general history and principles of local government in England. I have not included the many treatises on government in general, nor those on political economy, though, of course, in both these studies the question of the relationship of the central to local authorities is discussed. Mr. Mill's *Representative Government* (1861, 8vo) should be particularly consulted. Still there is not much to be said when one has digested all that is contained in the books specially devoted to the subject.

The archæological interest of the subject may be gathered from the following :—

Smith (Sir Thomas), The Commonwealth of England, and the manner and Government thereof, with new additions of the chiefe courts in England, and the offices thereof. London, printed by Will. Stansby for J. Smethwicke, and are to be sold at his shop in Saint Dunstanes Church-Yard. 1633. 12mo, 5 leaves, pp. 285.

This was first published in 1583, and many editions followed. The chapters relating to Local Government are as follows : Of the parts of Shires called Hundreds, Lathes, Rapes and Wapentakes, of the Court Baron, of the Leet or Law day, of the proceedings of causes criminall and first of the Justices of Peace, of Hue and Cry and Recognisance taken upon them that may give evidence, of the Coroners, of the Constables.

Officers : In this Boke is conteyned ye office of Shyriffes, Baylyffes of Lybertyes, Escheatours, Constables and Coroners, and shewethe what everye one of them may do by vertue of theyr offyces drawen out of bokes of the comen lawe of the statutes. Black letter, no date. 12mo, pp. 154 (not numbered).

Freeman (E. A.), Comparative Politics. London, 1873. 8vo, pp. ix, 522.

Gomme (George Laurence), Primitive Folk-Moots ; or, Open-air Assemblies in Britain. London, 1880. 8vo, pp. xi, 316. [An historical treatise on the earliest forms of local assemblies.]

On the history and development of local government the following are works of importance :—

Chalmers (M.D.) Local Government [The English Citizen : his rights and responsibilities]. London, 1883. 8vo, pp. viii, 160.

Contents :— Cap. i. Introductory. ii. General View. iii. The Parish. iv. The Union. v. The Municipal Borough. vi. The County. vii. The Sanitary District. viii. The School District. ix. The Highway Area. x. The Metropolis. xi. General Control.

Cobden Club Essays : Local Government and Taxation. Edited by J. W. Probyn. London, 1875. 8vo, pp. 454.

Contents :—Local Government in England, by Hon. George C. Brodrick.—Local

Government and Taxation in Scotland, by
Alexander M'Neel-Caird. — Local Government and Taxation in Ireland, by W. Neilson
Hancock.—Local Government and Taxation
in the Australian Colonies and New Zealand,
by Sir C. Dilke, Thomas Webb Ware and W.
H. Archer.—The Provincial and Communal
Institutions of Belgium and Holland, by Emile
de Laveleye.—Local Government in France,
by le Comte de Franqueville.—Local Govern-
ment and Taxation in Russia, by Ashton
Wentworth Dilke.—Local Government and
Taxation in Spain, by Señor Moret y Pren-
dergast.—Local Government considered in its
Historical Development in Germany and
England, with special reference to Recent
Legislation on the subject in Prussia, by R.
B. D. Morier.

Cobden Club Essays : Local Government and
Taxation in the United Kingdom. Edited
by J. W. Probyn. London, 1882. 8vo, pp. vi,
520.

Contents:—Local Government in England,
by the Hon. George C. Brodrick.—County
Boards, by C. T. D. Acland.—The Areas of
Rural Government, by Lord Edmond Fitz-
Maurice.—London Government, and how to
Reform it, by J. F. B. Firth.—Municipal
Boroughs and Urban Districts, by J. Thack-
ray Bunce.—Local Government and Taxation
in Ireland, by Richard O'Shaughnessy.—
Local Government and Taxation in Scotland,

by William Macdonald.—Local Taxation in England and Wales, by J. Roland Phillips.

Gneist (Dr. Rudolf), Geschichte und heutige Gestalt der Englischen Communalverfassung oder des Self-Government. Berlin, 1863. 2 vols. 8vo, pp. xxi, 682 ; 683-1398, and index 31 pp. [A valuable contribution to the history and statistics of local self-government in England.]

Contents : — Historical Development of the English Local Constitution.—Present Local Constitution in England and Wales : Jurisdiction and Officers, Local Taxation, Civil Jurisdiction of the County, Criminal and Police Constitution of the County, Municipal Constitution, Military, Parochial, Poor Law, Sanitary, Bridges and Highways, Law of Corporations.—Theory of Self-Government.

Smith (J. Toulmin), Local Self-Government and Centralisation : the characteristics of each, and its practical tendencies as affecting social, moral, and political welfare and progress, including comprehensive outlines of the English Constitution. London, 1851. 8vo, pp. vi, 409.

————— Local Self-Government Unmystified : a vindication of common sense, human nature, and practical improvements against the Manifesto of Centralism put forth at the Social Science Association, 1857. Second edition. London, 1857. 8vo, pp iv, 128.

On matters of statistics and modern facts
the most important works are :—

Goschen (George J.), Reports and Speeches on
  Local Government and Taxation. London,
  1872. 8vo, pp. vi, 218.

Local Government Board, Reports of the. Presented to both Houses of Parliament by
  command of Her Majesty. London, 1872-
  85. 14 vols., 8vo.

Local Taxation Returns [pursuant to Act 23 and
  24 Vict., c. 51]. Twenty parts, folio. House
  of Commons, 1862-81.

Local Taxes of the United Kingdom, containing a Digest of the Law, with a summary of
  statistical information concerning the several
  Local Taxes in England, Scotland, and Ireland. Published under the direction of the
  Poor - Law Commissioners. London, 1846
  pp. vi, 278

Rathbone (Wm.) and Sam. Whitbread, Local
  Government : Memorandum No. 1, General
  View; Memorandum No. 2, Law, with References. (Privately printed, 1877.) Two parts
  folio, pp. 42 ; 75. [These contain exceedingly
  valuable information, both of reference and
  of facts, which is arranged analytically under
  the following heads : (1) Existing Units of
  Local Government; (2) Matters which are
  Locally Administered ; (3) Local Taxation
  and Indebtedness.]

II.—THE SHIRE.

As long as we can historically speak of the old English "shire" we can think of the old independence of government within the shire. But when we have to speak of the "county" we find that local government is almost dead, replaced as it is by local autocracy. This was one of the chief works of the Norman conquest. A gathering of the shire gemote, such as that on Pennenden Heath, which met to do right between Lanfranc and Odo, could not be tolerated under the sovereignty of the Angevin kings, and representation had to give way to nomination. But the shire organisation has never entirely dropped out of our constitutional system. It has been made one of the chief instruments of administering justice, and in an extremely altered form has brought down to modern days some of its old traditional features.

Now that modern legislation is to step in and have its say on future shire government, why is it not possible to revert to the old names as well as to old forms? The future shire government will be representative and elective ; and as in old days it was representative and elective, there seems no reason why we should not go back to the names of old days, and speak of the " shire-moot" and not of the " county board."

The principal authorities on the history of the shire are Mr. Kemble, in his *Saxons in England* (vol. i, pp. 72-87), and Professor Stubbs, in his *Constitutional History of England* (vol. i, pp. 108-118). Sir Francis Palgrave, too, has much to say in his *History of the Rise and Progress of the English Commonwealth* (London, 1832); but it is scattered throughout his unindexed quarto volumes, and is not easily available. The Census Report of 1851 (vol. i) contains an exceedingly valuable introduction on the "Ancient Kingdoms and Provinces in England, Wales, and Scotland" (pp. lvi-lxxxii), from which we gain

some idea of the permanence of the boundaries during the period which has elapsed
since the Anglo-Saxon settlements. The
shires are evidently based upon the old

Beda.	Asser.	Saxon Chronicle before Alfred.	Saxon Chronicles after Alfred.
		Norðranhymbra land Suðanhymbra land	
Regio Loidis, or Elmet	Lincoln	Lindisware and Lindisse	Eorforwicscir Lindicolnascir
		Eastengle	East Engle
	Essex Kent	Eastseaxan Cantwara land [Merscware, the people of Romney Marsh)	Eastseaxe Cent
	Sussex	Su ðseaxan	Suð seaxe
	Surrey	Suðrige	Suðrige
Regio Sudergeona	Berkshire		Bearrucscir
Provincia Meanwarorun, Hundreds of East and West Meon	S'ampton	[Wiht (Isle of Wight)] Westseaxan	Hamtunscir
	Wilts Dorset Somerset Devon	Wilsaetan Dornsaetan Sumorsaetan	Wiltunscir Defenascir

divisions of the country, and the following
table, compiled from the early authorities,
will be found a useful key to the origin of
our modern shires.

Simeon of Durham.	Florence of Worcester and William of Malmesbury.	Modern Shire.
		Northumberland
		Durham
		Westmoreland
		Cumberland
		Lancashire
Eborascira		Yorkshire
Lincolnescira	Lincoln	Lincolnshire
Northfolc	Norfolk	Norfolk
Sudfolc	Suffolk	Suffolk
East saxe	Essex	Essex
Kent	Kent	Kent
Suthsexia	Sussex	Sussex
Suthrei	Surrey	Surrey
Berocscir	Berks	Berks
Sudhamtescir	Hants	Hants
Wiltescir	Wilts	Wilts
Dorsetescire	Dorset	Dorset
Somersetescire	Somerset	Somerset
Devenascire	Devon	Devon
	Cornwall	Cornwall
		Monmouth

Continued.

Beda.	Asser.	Saxon Chronicle before Alfred.	Saxon Chronicles after Alfred.
Middelangli Mercii Australes et Aquilonales		Myrcna land	Herefordscir scrobbesbyrigscir
			Deorabyscir Stæffordscir Snotingahamscir Legeceasterscir
Provincia Huicciorum }		Hwiccas {	Wigraceasterscir Gleawanceasterscir Wæringwicscir Hamtunscir
Regio Gyrwio- rum Australes Gyrwii			Huntandunscir Grantabrycgscir Oxnafordscir Buccingahamscir
		Middleseaxan	Bedanfordscir Heoitfordscir Middelseaxe

Without going into the interesting history which this table reveals, it may be
pointed out how clearly it confirms historical
opinion that the northern lands had no definite place in the English settlement until
late in Saxon times; that Cheshire has been
carved out of the *territorium* of the Roman
city of Chester; that Cornwall remained

Simeon of Durham.	Florence of Worcester and William of Malmesbury.	Modern Shire.
Herefordscira	Hereford	Hereford
Scrobscira	Shropshire	Shropshire
Cestrescira	Cheshire	Cheshire
Derbiscira	Derby	Derby
Steadfordscira	Stafford	Stafford
Snotinghamscira	Notts	Notts
Leorcestrescira	Leicester	Leicester
		Rutland
Wircestrescira	Worcester	Worcester
Gloucestrescira	Glou ester	Gloucester
Warewicscira	Warwick	Warwick
Norhamtunscira	Northants	Norhampton
Huntedunscira	Hunts	Huntingdon
Grantebrigescira	Cambridge	Cambridge
Oxenefordscira	Oxford	Oxford
Bukingeham- scira	Bucks	Bucks
Bedfordscira	Beds	Bedford
Hertfordscira	Herts	Herts
Midlesexa	Middlesex	Middlesex

impenetrably Celtic; and that Rutland and Monmouth[1] have altogether a modern history as English shires.

One curious archaic feature of the shires is well worth noting, because it undoubtedly

[1] The position of this county as an English shire has been worked out in the *Antiquary* (1881), vol. iv, pp. 91·96.

denotes very early influences, namely, isolated parts of one shire being locally
situated in another. The Act, 2 and 3
Will. IV, c. 64, sets out in a schedule a
number of the portions of counties which
were once isolated, and the Act, 7 and 8
Vict., cap. 61, did away with these anom-
alies. The subject has often been discussed
by the curious, and it is a feature that belongs to the early history of the English
shires, and probably tells us something
of the early migration of the conquering
races.

The later history of the shire, when,
indeed, it has become the county, is very
well summarised by Mr. Brodrick in the
volume of the *Cobden Club Essays.*

"By successive Acts of Parliament the
management of county affairs has been mainly
vested in the county magistrates. The more
important functions of county magistrates are
performed by them collectively at quarter
sessions, under the presidency of an unpaid
chairman elected by themselves. Of their
minor functions some can be performed by a
single magistrate, others by two magistrates
sitting together at petty sessions. But the

magistrates assembled at quarter sessions exercise a general control, by way of appeal or revision, over the action of individual magistrates, or of magistrates at petty sessions, and the standing committees of quarter sessions, through which they conduct most of their business, are practically so many little departments of state for the local government of counties.

" The criminal jurisdiction of the court of quarter sessions extends to all offences, except a few of the most aggravated.

" It may, therefore, be broadly stated, that county magistrates in quarter sessions have inherited the criminal jurisdiction, together with much of the administrative authority, which formerly belonged to the suitors of the old county courts, while the county magistrates, sitting without a jury in their several courts of petty sessions, have to a great extent taken the place of the popular hundred courts and courts-leet. On the other hand, the civil jurisdiction of the old county courts, having been obsolete for many generations, was revived by an Act of 1846, not in the court of quarter sessions, but in the new county courts, which are constituted on a wholly different principle. These courts are really nothing more than provincial branches of the imperial judicature, since their judges need have no qualification of county residence, and they are directed to be held in circuits which have no relation to county boundaries. They form, therefore, no part of county government, which in this respect as well as in others, is far less complete and self-contained than it was in Saxon times."[1]

The standard works on the office of Justice of the Peace are Richard Burn's *Justice of the Peace*, first published in 1754, continued by W. Woodfall, 4 vols., 8vo, 1805 ; Thomas Walter Williams's *Justice of the Peace*, enlarged by H. Nuttall Tomlins, 4 vols., 8vo, 1812 ; and J. F. Archbold's *Justice of the Peace and Parish Officer*, 5th edit., 4 vols., 1824-5, 12mo. There is a useful article, giving the history of the office, in the *Penny Cyclopædia*, xiii, 158-160, as well as in Knight's *English Cyclopædia*, "Arts and Sciences", v, 33. Consult also John Clarke's *Bibliotheca Legum ; or a complete Catalogue of the Common and Statute Law-books of the United Kingdom*, ed. 1819, 8vo. Burn's *Justice of the Peace* is arranged alphabetically, and many of the entries in its earliest editions are exceedingly curious

---

[1] *Local Government and Taxation, England*, Brodrick, pp. 32 3.

and instructive upon county, legal, and
social antiquities. The first edition of this
noted book belongs to that unenviable
class which enrich the publisher and bring
no gain to the author—it was sold for a
few pounds.

There is a great deal of interesting personal history connected with county government, a very good specimen of which was
given by Mr. Edward Peacock in the *Antiquary*, 1882 (vol. v, pp. 159-160), on the
Lindsey Justices of the Peace, *temp.* Henry
VIII; in which article Mr. Peacock draws
attention to the importance of publishing
the important documents connected with
this subject.

All the shires have found an historian of
more or less capability,[1] and in most of them
there exists an archæological society which
publishes from time to time volumes rela-
ing to the history and antiquities of the
district. But it is curious how very little

---

[1] These may be ascertained very readily from Mr.
Anderson's *Book of British Topography*, a very valuable aid to the local historian.

work has been done towards writing the corporate history of each county. In point of fact, it may be said that up to this time nothing has been attempted in this direction. Materials are now, however, rapidly accumulating and being made accessible. The magistrates of Middlesex have allowed their papers to be calendared, and a Middlesex County Record Society has been formed to publish these valuable papers, and so make them available for general use. The prospectus states—

"The county of Middlesex possesses a collection of old records relating to its civil and criminal history which, commencing in the year 1549 (the third of Edward VI), and continuing to the present time, covers with more or less completeness a period of 335 years. Only in Essex and the North Riding of Yorkshire do the records date from so early a period as in Middlesex.

"Quite recently, the old county records (including in that category all up to the close of the reign of George III) have been placed in a newly-constructed Muniment Room at the Sessions House, Clerkenwell, and have been arranged, labelled, and indexed by order of the Court of Quarter Sessions. This important work has been carried out, at a cost to the county of more than a thousand pounds, under the advice and supervision of Mr. Cordy Jeaffreson, who was in the first instance deputed by the Historical MSS. Commissioners to examine and report upon the records; and they are now for the first time made practically available for investigation and use.

"The various classes of records, form a collection of upwards of ten thousand volumes, and nearly five thousand rolls or bundles, each of which contains numerous separate documents. They may be briefly stated to include:—

"1.—A series of sessions rolls almost complete, except in some of the earlier years, from Edward VI to 1820, of which Mr. Jeaffreson remarks :—'Something more should, however, be said of the contents of the sessions rolls, that comprise considerably more than half a million separate writings, in recognisances, indictments, and inquisitions *post mortem.* It having been the usage of the clerks of the Middlesex Justices, from the time of Elizabeth, to put at the foot of each recognisance a brief note of the matter to which the document referred, and of the purpose for which the obligation was created, the recognisances of the Middlesex Sessional Archives afford a larger measure of entertainment and historical information than one would expect to gather from writings of their class. A considerable minority of these footnotes yield some interesting particulars of the social manners, domestic interests, political ferments, and religious agitations of Londoners in olden time. In the fewest possible words they tell the story of a playhouse riot, a destructive fire, the arrest of a Jesuit, a daring burglary at Whitehall, the great plate robbery of the year, or an outbreak of the London apprentices. They exhibit by turns the humour of the court and the humour of the tavern, the pomp of a noble's palace and the cheer of a modest home, the tricks of the professional cardsharper and the cunning ways of tradesmen. And these notes are the more deserving of attention because they often refer to matters that, either from being dealt with summarily, or from being dropped for want of sufficient evidence, do not reappear with greater preciseness and amplitude in the indictments of the subsequent bundles. From some of the memoranda curious particulars may be gleaned respecting robberies committed in the dwellings of persons stricken by the great plague, and the dread of incendiaries and makers of explosive compounds that seized the Londoners immediately after the great fire of Charles the Second's time ; respecting the temper and excesses of the Sacheverell rioters ; and respecting the demeanour of the London Jacobites, *temp.* Anne and George I. Some of the indictments are especially worthy of examination. A careful manipulator of these sources of evidence could extort a large addition to the materials for England's religious history, from the records of the presentments of Catholic recusants in the earlier decades, and the prosecutions of the Protestant Dissenters in the later decades of the seventeenth century. From the indictments for seditious libels he would also recover to English literature the heart and life of many a curious tract that perished in the Stuart period, in flames kindled by the common hangman.'

" 2.—Sessions books, commencing 1639, containing records of sentences passed upon prisoners ; orders relating to the various parishes of the county ; addresses to the sovereigns, etc., etc., forming a series of 1,775 volumes, from which much information of value can be gleaned.

" 3.--Process books of indictments, from 1610 to 1775, containing many interesting entries, including the names of persons fined for not taking the sacrament.

" 4.—Oath rolls, 1660 to 1820, containing oaths of allegiance, supremacy, and abjuration ; declarations against transubstantiation; associations in the reign of William III ; clergy oath rolls ; entries of the meeting places of Dissenters ; etc., etc.

" 5.—Registers of the estates of Papists, 1675 to 1764.

" 6.- Justices' certificates of convictions and appeals for holding conventicles, 1664—1687. Files of proceedings against Dissenters charged with being present at religious exercises other than those appointed by the Church of England, ' constituting a body of evidences of the highest

D

interest and importance to the historian of Anglican Nonconformity in London.'

"7.—Sacramental certificates. Many thousands of certificates from 1671 to 1825, containing the names and autographs of very many eminent Englishmen, and of clergy of the London parishes.

"8.—Justices' certificates of non-jurors, recusants, etc., from 1673, giving the names. professions, trades, places of abode, etc., of those who were summoned and appeared, or failed to appear, of those who subscribed the rolls or refused to do so, etc.

"9.—Hearth and stove tax accounts, 1664, a complete set, 'of great importance to the genealogist.'

"10.—List of freeholders liable to serve on juries in the various parishes and places of the county, in fifteen folio volumes, continuous from 1696 to 1789 ; commissions of the peace, etc., 1687 to 1785 ; register of the estates of justices, 1746 to 1820 ; etc., etc.

"11.—Orders of Council concerning the plague, 1661 to 1666. This book also contains lists of recusants, persons fined for "prophane language," cursing and swearing, etc.

"12.—Orders of Court made at Quarter Sessions, from 1716. A series full of interesting information of the proceedings of the justices touching the government of the county in its various departments.

"13.—Land tax accounts. A series extending from 1767 to 1833. Most useful in pedigree enquiries.

"14.—Miscellanea. Lists of alehouses at various periods, the earliest being 1552 ; lists of butchers' recognisances against selling meat in Lent, 1631 ; books and contracts relating to county works, *e.g.*, bridges, prisons, the New Sessions House, Clerkenwell, the paving of the Haymarket, maintenance of the streets, etc., etc., from George I ; books relating to the Militia, 1757—1816 ; and many others."

The whole forming (in Mr. Jeaffreson's words) " a body of Muniments which would enable a zealous and competent antiquary to produce an adequate history of the county, from Elizabeth to Victoria."[1]

Again, the Justices of the North Riding of Yorkshire have taken steps for the better preservation of their records. With that view they asked the help of the Historical MSS. Commission, and Mr. Jeaffreson, who has been doing like work on the West Riding muniments, was deputed to draw up a report on the historical worth of the records. These documents go back to the beginning of Elizabeth's reign, and contain much matter of local and personal interest, especially pertaining to the Catho-

[1] Cf. a paper in the *Gentleman's Magazine* for 1860, part ii, p. 123.

lics and their estates. Other counties are.
following the same line. The arrangement
of the Essex County Records, kept at
Chelmsford, has just been brought to com-
pletion (1885). A proper record room has
been provided for their preservation, and
the various series of rolls and loose documents have been classified and ticketed.
The sessions rolls commence in the reign
of Elizabeth, and form the leading class,
but the various groups of records usually
found in county collections are also well
represented. The documents relating to
recusancy are full of interest. "Inasmuch
as tradition, if not better evidence, says
that when they were in Springfield Gaol
barrowloads of these very records were used
for manure (!), it is matter for congratula-
tion that this county has any records left
to arrange."—*Athenæum.*

On the general functions of county government we have the following works, all
of which are much more than mere curious
law treatises :—

Boke (The) for a Justyce of Peace neuer so wel and dylygently set forthe. Black letter. London: Robert Redman, n.d. 12mo, fol. 51 and tabula.

Lambard (W.), Justice of the Peace. 1619. 4to.

Dalton (M.), Country Justice. Third edition. 1626. 4to.

Horne (Andrew), The Booke called the Mirrour of Justices, made by Andrew Horne; with the book calld The Diversity of Courts, and their Jurisdictions. Both translated out of the Old French in the English tongue by William Hughes. London, 1646. 12mo, 14 leaves, pp. 325 and the table.

Another edition : London, 1768. 8vo.

Another edition : Manchester, 1840. 8vo, pp. xx, 262.

Greenwood (William), The Authority, Jurisdiction and Method of Keeping County Courts, Courts-Leet, and Courts-Baron ; explaining the judicial and ministerial authority of Sheriffs, also the office and duty of a Coroner. Eighth edition. [London] in the Savoy, 1722. 8vo, pp. ii, 486, the table.

Justices of the Peace. *Gentleman's Magazine*, 1788, i, p. 315 ; ii, 675-6 ; 856-7.

Acland (Charles T. D.), County Boards. *Fortnightly Review*, 1881, vol. xxix, pp. 93-102.

Some most important information is to be

gained from a parliamentary blue book issued in 1868, with a good index, and now very scarce, entitled,

Report from the Select Committee of the House of Commons on County Financial Arrangements.

Historically, very suggestive contributions to the subject will be found in—

Goldsmid (Augustus), On Hungarian Political and County Institutions, and their analogy to our own. *Journ. Arch. Ass.*, vol. xxviii, pp. 241-244.

Hamilton (A. H. A.), Quarter Sessions from Queen Elizabeth to Queen Anne. 1878. 8vo.

Special counties have been treated of in the following works :—

Brockett (John T.), Extracts from the Minute Book in the Clerk of Assizes Office for the Northern Circuit, 1665 to 1675. *Archæologia Æliana*, vol. iii, 4to, pp. 86-92.

General Report to the King in Council from the Honourable Board of Commissioners on the Public Records. Vol. xv, large folio, 1837.

Contains reports upon the following county records : Circuits—City of London, Midland,

Norfolk, Northern, Oxford, the Great Ses-
sions of Wales, Brecon. Counties Palatine—
Durham, Lancashire. Clerks of the Peace—
Berkshire, Cheshire, Cornwall, Cumberland,
Derby, Durham, Essex, Hereford, Lancaster,
Leicester, Lincoln, Monmouth, Northampton,
Northumberland, Nottingham, Oxford, Salop,
Stafford, Suffolk, Sussex, Warwick, Worces-
ter, Cardigan, Caermarthen, Denbigh, Gla-
morgan, Merioneth, Montgomery, Pembroke,
Radnor. County Registries — Middlesex,
Yorkshire.

Anglesey :

Breese (Edward), Kalendars of Gwynedd ; or,
Chronological Lists of the Lords-Lieutenants,
Custodes Rotulorum, Sheriffs, and Knights of
the Shire for the counties of Anglesey,
Caernarvon, and Merioneth. London, 1873.
4to.

Carmarthen :

Phillips (John Roland), A List of the Sheriffs
of Cardiganshire from A.D. 1539 to A.D. 1868,
with genealogical and historical notes. Carmarthen, 1868. 8vo.

Cheshire :

Black (W. H.), On the Records of the County
Palatine of Chester. *Journ. Arch. Ass.*, vol.
v, pp. 187-195.

Jolley (John), The Head-Constable's Assistant;
or, a Mize-Book for the County-Palatine of

Cheshire : the same being Tables ready cast up ; whereby any Township's just proportion of any Tax charged by way of the Mize may readily and exactly be known. London, 1726. 8vo.

Yates (Joseph Brooks), The Rights and Jurisdiction of the County Palatine of Chester. the Earls Palatine, the Chamberlain, and other officers. Printed in the *Chetham Miscellany*, vol. ii, pp. 37.

Devon :

Hamilton (A. H. A.), Justices of the Peace for the County of Devon under Charles I and Oliver Cromwell. *Transactions of the Devonshire Association*, vol. x, pp. 309-314.

Worth (R. N.), The Common Seals of Devon. *Transactions of the Devonshire Association*, vol. vi, pp. 79-100, 686-688 ; vol. viii, p. 269.

Lancashire :

Lancashire Lieutenancy under the Tudors and Stuarts : the Civil and Military Government of the County, as illustrated by a series of Royal Letters, Orders of the Privy Council, the Lord-Lieutenant, etc. Edited by John Harland, F.S.A. Chetham Society, 1859. 2 vols., 4to.

Lincolnshire :

Chronological Tables of the High Sheriffs of the County of Lincoln. London, 177y. 8vo.

Middlesex :

Hawkins (Sir J.), A Dissertation on the Armorial
Ensigns of the County of Middlesex. 1780.

Norfolk :

Vicecomites Norfolciæ ; or, Sheriffs of Norfolk
from the first year of Henry the Second to
the fourth year of Queen Victoria inclusive ;
chronologically and alphabetically arranged,
with their armorial bearings. Stow Bardolph.
1843. 4to.

Northumberland :

Dickson (William), The Wards, Divisions,
Parishes, and Townships of Northumberland,
according to the ancient and modern divisions.
Alnwick, 1833. 4to.

Oxfordshire :

Davenport (J. M.), Lords-Lieutenant and High
Sheriffs of Oxfordshire, 1086-1868. Oxford,
1868. 8vo.

Renfrewshire :

Hector (William), Selections from the Judicial
Records of Renfrewshire, with notes, and six
facsimiles of old documents. Paisley, 1876.
8vo.

Somersetshire :

Reports of the Royal Commission on Historical
Manuscripts, presented to both Houses of
Parliament by command of Her Majesty.
London, 1874-1881. Folio, 8 vols.

Contains reports on the county records of Somerset, iii, 333-334 ; vii, 693-701.

Wilts :

Jackson (J. E.), The Sheriff's Tourn, county Wilts, A.D. 1439.   Devizes, 1872.   8vo.

Yorkshire :

Atkinson (J. C.), Quarter Sessions Records [vol. i, part i, of the North Riding Record Society's publications], 1884.   8vo, pp. 160.

III.—THE HUNDRED.

THERE is very great obscurity as to the origin of the territorial divisions known as hundreds. The territorial nature of the division meets us in the peculiar use of the word shire. Cornwall is professedly divided into shires, not hundreds, the modern hundreds of Trigg and East, for instance, being mentioned as Triconscire[1] and Estwyveleshire;[2] and in Yorkshire we have Borgheshire, Craveshire, Richmondshire, Riponshire, Hallamshire, Islandshire, and Norhamshire ; and it is not very much beyond historical proof that the next higher local division to the township was originally known as shire.[3] Without entering, then,

[1] In Alfred's Will. See Stubbs's *Const. Hist.*, i, 100.

[2] *Hist. MSS. Com.*, vi, 524.

[3] Stubbs' *Const. Hist.*, i, 100. The term "shrift shire" (Wilkins's *A.-S. Laws*, p. 83. secs. 6, 9, 15 ; *Thorpe*, vol. ii. pp. 245, 246) is used, not parish, to

into the question of the connection between
the hundred of Tacitus and the hundred to
be met with in English history, we may
safely state that its place in the early history of local government was immediately
above the township, the union of a number
of which, for the purpose of judicial administration, peace, and defence, formed the
hundred.[1]

The oldest aspect of the hundred is military, and this has lasted down to our own
days. It is very probable that the colonists
of Britain arranged themselves in hundreds
of warriors; and, in later ages, the new

express the range within which the priest fulfils his
duties. Late translators have, indeed, but in the
teeth of the plain meaning, given this word the form
" parochia." Bede, again, has a term which King
Alfred renders "mynster-shire", *Hist. Eccles.*, lib. 5,
cap. xix, which compare with (*e.g.*) lib. iii, cap. xix;
and see King Alfred's translation of these passages.
Bosworth's *A.-S. Dictionary*, p. 245; and see "Preost
Shire," p. 278.—Toulmin Smith's *The Parish*, p. 240.

[1] There are a great number of authorities as to the
origin of the hundred; but the best English works
are Stubbs' *Const. Hist.*, i, pp. 96 101 ; *Kemble*, cap.
ix, book i; Palgrave's *Eng. Com.*, vol. i, pp. 97 *et seq.*;
Census Returns, 1851, Report, pp. lxii-lxv ; Ellis's
Introd. to Domes., i, 187, 188.

territorial hundred was the basis upon
which military levies were made.[1] Now,
in the hundred warriors of early times, we
must not understand an indiscriminate levy
of persons to serve in an artificially formed
army : they were the picked champions,
the representatives of a hundred families.[2]
And, moreover, a hundred families who
recognised a common inheritance and bond
of union with each other ; who ranged
themselves together under one name and
for common political and religious purposes.

The early historical significance of the
hundred is to be tested by a comparison of
it with the wapentake. A law of Æthel-
red II is at great pains to define the constitution and functions of the gemote or
judicial assembly of the wapentakes of
the north of England, yet there can be
little doubt of the existence of the wapen-

---

[1] See throughout, *Hist. MSS. Reports*, *e.g.* v, 422,
and vi, 347, *temp*. Chas. I.

[2] The Swats reckon the number of their inhabi-
tants by the number of matchlocks. See Bengal As.
Soc. *Journ.*, No. iii, 1862, p. 270 ; cf. Toulmin
Smith's *The Parish*, p. 18.

take court very long before the time of
that monarch. The wapentake answers in
every respect to the hundred (Ellis's *Introduction to Domesday*), but its northern
terminology is much more expressive than
that of the southern hundred. An interesting passage from Ellis's *Introduction to
Domesday* bears upon this point, and is
worth quoting.

The wapentake occurs in the northern
counties, and is synonymous with the hundred in the counties of Nottingham, York,
and Lincoln to this day. The best explanation of the wapentake is given in the
laws of King Edward the Confessor : " De
Hundredis et Wapentachiis. Ewerwick-
shire, Nicolscyre (Lincolnshire), Noting-
hamshyre, Leycestershire, Northampton-
shire, usque ad Watlingstrete, et octo mili-
aria ultra Watlingstrete sub lege Anglorum
sunt. Et quod Angli vocant Hundredum,
supradicti comitatus vocant Wapentachi-
um : et non sine causa : cum quis enim
accipiebat præfecturam Wapentachii, die
statuto in loco ubi consueverant congregari,

omnes majores natu contra eum conveniebant, et descendente eo de equo suo omnes assurgebant ei. Ipse vero erecta lancea sua ab omnibus secundum morem fœdus accipiebat : omnes enim quotquot venissent cum lanceis suis ipsius hastam tangebant, et ita se confirmabant per contactum armorum, pace palam concessa. Anglice enim arma vocantur wæpnu, et taccane confirmare ; quasi armorum confirmatio vel, ut magis expresse secundam linguam Anglicam dicamus Wapentac, armorum tactus est ; pæpnu enim arma sonat, tac tactus est. Quamobrem potest cognosci quod hac de causa totus ille conventus dicitur Wapentac eo quod per tactum armorum suorum ad invicem confœderati sunt." (Wilkins' *Leges Anglo-Sax.*, p. 203.)

Ranulphus Cestrensis tells us (lib. i, cap. 5; see Cowell; compare also *Chron., Joan. Bromton*, ap. x, Script Twysd, p. 957) : " Quod quoties novus esset Hundredi Dominus ei in subjectionis signum arma redderent Vassalli :" an explanation which, in some measure, connects the English wapen-

take with the wapinschaw, or wapinschaw-
ing, of the Scots." (Jamieson's *Ety. Dic. of
Scot. Lang.*)

That the wapentake was one of the earliest terms used by the Saxons in this country
for a district of territory, seems more than
probable. It may be traced among the
more ancient tribes of the north. Professor
Ihre tells us that among the Goths wapntak implied the manner in which decrees
were passed by the people at large, by the
clashing of their arms. Tacitus, he adds,
has described the usage in his time. He
further informs us that wapntak also de-
noted the confirmation of a judicial edict
by the touch of arms. The votes being
collected, the judge reached forth a spear,
by touching which all his assessors confirmed the sentence.

"Wapntak erat modus per strepitum
concussorum armorum plebiscita olim con-
dendi, uti recte hanc vocem explicat Dol-
merus" (in *Notis ad Jus. Aul. Norrw.*, p. 9;
conf. Heims' *Kr.*, tom. ii, p. 313). "Their
bardo saman wapnom sinom, oc dœmdo tha

alla utlaga, arma sua concutiebant, omnes-
que eos exsules esse jusserunt" (*ib.* p. 414).
" Arni beiddi, at men skuldo gera wapnatak
at Thui, at dæma med lagum Sigurd Jarl oc
allam flock Theirra til fiandans : Arni ad
populum ferebat, ut concussis armis ple-
biscitoque publico Sigurdum comitem om-
nesque sectarios illius diabolo adjudicarent"
(*Adde Knytl*, s. p. 44). " Rem suo jam ævo
usitatem describit" (*Tacitus de Mor. Germ.*,
cap. xi). Dr. Wilkins, in his *Glossary* upon
the Anglo-Saxon laws, derives " wapentake"
from " weapan arma" and "teacan docere,"
as the district where a given number of
persons in each county were accustomed to
meet and train themselves in the use of
arms (Wilkins's *Leg. Ang.-Sax.*, p. 117 ;
see also *Chron., Joan Bromton*, apud x,
Script. Twysd, 895 ; Ellis's *Introd. to
Domes.*, i, 181, 182, 183).

The muster rolls of the hundred recall
the concilium of Tacitus, where every
citizen was a soldier, and every soldier a
citizen. They come down to so late a
period as the time of Charles the First.

E

A general muster is attended by all the inhabitants of a hundred;[1] and a warrant of one of Cromwell's generals desires the constables to summon all the men of the hundred of Williton to appear before him in complete arms on a certain day.[2]

There is an interesting fact to be noticed before passing to the hundred as a territorial division of the country. Most of the names of the modern hundreds are not repeated in the names of the townships. If the hundred is derived from the old personal organisation, this is exactly what we might expect. The names of the ancient personal hundreds would be derived from some tribal or clan chief who led the ancient families making up the hundreds; and the names of the territorial hundreds so far meet this view as to be to a great extent independent names of territory at the present day. Thus, Lincoln comprises 29 wapentakes, of which 20 have distinctive names that do not appear in the list of

[1] See the Muster Booke of all the inhabitants of the hundred of Llyvou, *Hist. MSS. Com.*, v, 422.
[2] *Ibid.*, vi, 347.

towns. In Yorkshire, East Anglia, and the north midland counties, the names have the same character : 18 of 27 names of wapentakes in Yorkshire, 20 of 30 names of hundreds in Norfolk ; 18 of 21 names in Suffolk, are not derived from any of their townships ; in the shires of Stafford, Worcester, Warwick, Leicester, Rutland, Nottingham, Derby, Northumberland, and Cumberland, the hundreds and wards have not been derived from the names of towns; and taking the whole of England, there are only 362 out of 799 names of hundreds, wapentakes, or liberties the same as names of towns (*Census Report*, 1851, p. lxiv). Considering how varied the names of the present hundreds are compared with those mentioned even so late as Domesday (Ellis *Introd. Domes.*, i, 34), this result is, I think, significant enough to place it on record.[1]

---

[1] I communicated to *Notes and Queries*, 5th Ser., ix, p. 403, an example of a scheme, which I have since improved upon, for a tabular view of the history of the hundreds.

All the judicature lying outside the village system was centred in the hundred. It was entitled to declare folk-right in every suit ; its jurisdiction was criminal as well as civil, and voluntary as well as contentious. It tried criminals, settled disputes, and witnessed transfers of land (Stubbs, *Const. Hist.*, i, 104).

Adding to this the two instances mentioned by Sir Henry Ellis (*Introd. to Domes.*, i, 188) of land assigned to a hundred being changed by a verdict of the men of the hundred, in the *Domesday* accounts of Gloucestershire and Bedfordshire, I think we have some valuable evidence of the ancient legislative functions of the hundred-court.

The remaining feature of the hundred-court which we have now to examine is the executive. As a civil and criminal court of justice its judicial capacity was no doubt in the early times very extensive. No suit could be taken to a higher court until first it had been tried in the hundred-court. Its hundreds-ealdor is directed by the laws of Edgar (iv, 8, 10) to be the referee in questions of witness ; and he is probably a distinct officer from the hundred-man, who with his tithing-men go forth to execute justice on the thief (*Ibid.*, i, 2, 4, 5).

The court was held once a month, and was attended by all the fully qualified free-men. Among the Franks and Lombards a very significant term was applied to this body of suitors, namely, *rachimburgi*, which Savigny derives from *rek*, rich or great, and *burg*, surety. It betokens that some sort of superiority belonged to those who attended the hundred-court over those who did not attend ; and it betokens, more-over, that the fact of a certain portion of men of the hundred having ceased to attend the hundred-court, had entered into the politics of the age, and had, therefore, impressed itself on the political phraseology of the age.

The general reluctance to attend is proved, in the reign of Henry I at all events, by documentary evidence, namely the entrances of fines in the pipe-roll,

(Stubbs, *Const. Hist.*, i, 398). This non-attendance brings about a clear distinction between the old popular hundred assembly and the new hundred-court. The shrinking up of the old assembly into a committee, so to speak, of twelve members, to transact the judicial business of the court, began very soon. Among the Franks, the smaller body was called the sitting *rachimburgs*, in opposition to the rest, who are the standing members (Stubbs, i, 54) ; and the parallels in England I cannot doubt to be the great court, or sheriff's tourn, or leet, as it was afterwards called, held twice a year, and the curia parva Hundredi, held every three weeks, which, though appearing now to be so distinct from each other, belonged originally to the old hundred assembly—the one representing the civil, the other the criminal, jurisdiction of the hundred-moot.

The hundred-courts were not only not abolished, but were directed to be held regularly, and non-attendance upon them was punished by fines. Moreover, the sheriff's tourn and leet, as it was called, a court which so long exercised the same kind of criminal jurisdiction as that now vested in the magistrates, was but the hundred-court under another and less popular name. Yet these courts rapidly lost their importance, partly because they were superseded by the county-courts, now held monthly, and partly because so many franchises, or rights of private jurisdiction, had been attached by grants to lordships, as greatly to reduce and obstruct the business of the smaller popular courts.[1]

The legislative functions of the hundred assembly passed away with its independence, as the military concilium of the early Teutons. When the local assemblies had ceased to be sovereign, the business must always have been mainly judicial (Freeman, *Comp. Polit.,* p. 243). Accordingly, we have an excess of the executive element from the very beginning of the history of the hundred-court. The legislative element, however, does appear, even under the

---

[1] *Local Government and Taxation,* Cobden Club, England, Broderick, p. 11.

altered jurisdiction of the hundred-court. We find it in the formal acceptance or rejection of the taxation demands ; in the form of the muster rolls for the supply of soldiers ; and in some special cases where the courts of the great franchises still exist in something like their original form, being less touched than the hundred-courts themselves by general legislation. There are several instances among the local records of a hundred having rejected, after deliberation, the precept served upon them for taxes ; and Toulmin Smith mentions an instance where Parliament is petitioned by two hundreds for some redress with reference to recent taxation (*The Parish,* p. 20).

Interesting and important as this subject is to the constitutional historian, we find really that very little attention has been given to it outside the general treatises on constitutional history. Already I have enumerated in a note the best general authorities. Besides these it may be noted that the meeting places of the hundred-courts are treated of in my *Primitive Folk-moots.*

Mr. Seebohm, in his *Village Community in
England*, has drawn attention to some interesting phases of the history of the hundred.
Mr. Eyton, in his *Domesday Studies: Somerset* (London, 1880, 2 vols., 4to), and *Key to
Domesday: Analysis of the Dorset Survey*
(4to, 1877), gives much valuable information
with reference to those two counties. But
the list of books and papers upon this section of our subject is very meagre.

Rotuli Hundredorum temp. Hen. III et Edw. I
in turr' Lond' et in curia receptæ scaccarii
Westm. asservati. Printed by command of
H.M. King George III. 1812. 2 vols., folio.
Pp. 16, 700 ; ix, 1101.
  Vol. I. Articuli ad inquirend'—Rotulorum
Hundredorum exemplar—Bedford'—Berk'—
Buck'—Cantebr'—Cornub'— Derb' — Devon'
Dorset' — Ebor'— Essex—Glouc'— Heref—
Hertf'- Huntedon'—Kanc'— Leycestr'—Lin-
coln'—Civit' Lond'—Com' North—Comitatus
Northfolch—Index Locorum—Index Nomi-
num.
  Vol. II. Norht' — Northt' — Northumbr'—
Notingh'm—Oxon —Rotelond—Salop— Staf-
ford—Sum'set—Suffolc— Sussex—Suth'mtes
—Warrwyk' — Wyltes' (Henry III)—Wylt'
(Edw. I)—Wygorn—Derb'—Noting'—Bede-

ford'— Buk'— Cantabr'— Hunt'— Oxon'—
Index Locorum—Index Nominum.

Modus tenendi unum hundredum sive curiam
de recordo. Robert Redman, London, 1539.
12mo.

On the Ancient Division of Counties into Hundreds. *Gentleman's Magazine*, 1828, pp.
99-102.

Barnes (Rev. William) On the Origin of the
Hundred and Tithing of English Law.
*Journal of the British Archæological Associa-
tion*, vol. xxviii, pp. 21-27.

Coote (Henry Charles), The Milites Station-
arii considered in relation to the Hundred
and Tithing of England. *Archæologia*, xliv.

Archæologia Cantiana : Extract from the Hundred Rolls, vii, 322.

Lightfoot (W. F.) Documents relating to a
dispute between the Seven Hundreds and
Lydd concerning the Watch at Denge Marsh,
from MS. *Arch. Cant.*, viii, 299-310.

Mayer (Joseph) On the Arming of Levies in the
Hundred of Wirral, in the County of Chester,
and the introduction of small fire-arms as
weapons of war in place of bows and arrows.
Liverpool, 1859. 8vo.

Subsidy Roll for the Hundred of Faversham,
14 Henry VIII. London, 1878. 8vo.

IV.—MUNICIPAL GOVERNMENT.

OF all forms of local government the most vigorous is that incidental to the municipal borough. Whether it be that Roman influences have been at work on English soil to a greater extent than is at present recognised, or whether it be that the English branch of the Aryan race has followed, in a considerably modified degree, though on exactly the same principle, the constitutional instinct which is portrayed in early Greek life, the fact remains that the municipal borough has lent itself to the requirements of succeeding ages far more effectually than either the shire, the hundred, or even the parish. There are marked associations with the history of municipal institutions which, unfortunately, have hitherto impeded a thorough penetration to the early history of English municipal towns, and, indeed, have suggested, if not asserted, that there is no such early history at all ; nothing prior to the assumption of municipal rights and privileges. These associations may be thus grouped : the idea that everything municipal has been derived from Rome ;[1] that the charter granted by the king, or other lord, is the commencing point of the known history of English municipal towns ;[2] that municipal history occupies a position quite apart from and independent of all other local institutions.

In dealing with a definite set of institutions like that of municipal corporations, it is certainly well to ascertain what place they occupy in the polity of the nation. Are they of purely modern growth ? Have they exercised any special influences on the

---

[1] Pearson's *Early and Middle Ages of England*, i, 264 ; Mr. Wright, in *Archæologia*, vol. xxxii ; and *Celt, Roman and Saxon;* Coote's *Romans of Britain*, 359-382.

[2] Hallam, *Europe during Middle Ages*, p. 571, *n.* (Murray), says that he is unable to discover any trace of internal self-government before the granting of charters. Robertson, *Charles V*, vol. i, p. 33, says that corporations were introduced after the Conquest from France.

political history of the nation? Have
they a place in the wide field of comparative politics? These are some of the
primary questions to which just now an
appeal is being made to English history.
The citadel fortresses of the early Britons,
proudly enumerated by Nennius, were,
there can be little doubt, brought quickly
under Roman subjugation, and either destroyed or utilised; the exact proportion of
these two alternatives being perhaps capable
of measurement by the extreme difficulty
of identifying, except in such special cases
as York, Chester, Lincoln, Leicester, Norwich, Carmarthen, London, Canterbury,
and some others, the Roman occupation of
the old British site. But what then has
become of the Roman cities? Mr. Freeman
puts it in this way, that "it seems quite certain that the English seldom, if ever, at
once occupied a Roman or British town.
The towns were commonly forsaken for a
while, though they were in many cases re-
settled by an English population."[1] It is

---

[1] *History of Norman Conquest,* vol. i, p. 15.

not worth while, and of course it is not
possible within our present limits, to go
over the whole ground covered by this proposition, but it is to be observed that it is
just at this stage that all inquirers into the
early history of municipal institutions have
stumbled : they see in this re-occupation of
a Roman city a resuscitation of Roman
municipal polity; or they boldly answer
Mr. Freeman's continuation of the above-
quoted sentence—" the only question is
whether the towns, in any cases, preserved
a sort of half-independence after the conquest of the surrounding country "[1]—by
asserting that the independence was real
and not half-hearted ; that here, if anywhere, Roman life and Roman polity have,
by unbroken descent, influenced English
life and English polity. But fully recog-
nising the uneven ground of the early
English settlement in Britain, there is yet
evidence enough to show that the fight with
Rome, even in her cities, was a fight which

[1] Mr. Freeman speaks more decisively in *Norman
Conquest,* v, 470.

ended in the birth of English municipal institutions, as well as English village institutions.

It is important to note that of the existing municipalities of England, only comparatively few occupy the same sites as the Roman municipia, or colonia, mentioned by Ptolemy and Nennius, or even as the stations mentioned in the *Antonine Itinerary*, the *Notitia*, and by the *Ravenna Geographer;* but, though London, York, Lincoln, Leicester, Canterbury, and Winchester have a continuous historical existence in these authorities, they wisely do not venture (to use the words of Professor Stubbs[1]), like some of the towns of southern France, to claim an unbroken succession from the Roman municipality. Though Verulamium, Caistor, Dunium, and Etocetum find a place throughout these early historians, St. Albans, Norwich, Dorchester, and Lichfield rear themselves on or alongside those old Roman sites, without, so far as history teaches us, deriving any advantage

[1] *Const. Hist.*, i, 62.

from Roman institutions.[1] Again, Wrox-
eter, Cirencester,[2] Silchester. Catarac,
though mentioned by the same authorities,
disappear as boroughs at and since the time
of *Domesday;* while Ludlow, Marlborough,
Doncaster, Carlisle, and Farnham, all mentioned either in *Ptolemy* or the *Antonine
Itinerary,* are not municipal boroughs until
long after *Domesday.*[3] Such are a few examples of the broken line of progress which
towns, known to have had a Roman organisation, either as municipia or colonia, have
made in England. The causes thereof, however difficult to trace and gather together
into a historical narrative, can at once be
stated not to belong to the Roman influence
by which the towns were created: that would,
on the contrary, have produced a uniform
progress, a strongly marked topographical

---

[1] *Vide* Thompson's *Eng. Mun. Hist.,* pp. 91, 110.
[2] Cirencester is mentioned as a borough in 1399,
but disappears again after that time.
[3] The dates are as follows: Ludlow, 1300; Marlborough, 1200; Doncaster, 1194; Carlisle, Henry
III; Farnham, 1310. See tables affixed to Merewether and Stephen's *Hist. of Mun. Corp.,* vol. iii.

whole body of burgesses was called upon to sanction the measures which interested the community. The difficulty of conducting business in such an assembly seems to have suggested the expedient of appointing a species of committee out of the larger body, which acted in conjunction with the burgesses, and which was dissolved when the business was concluded. These committees afterwards became permanent. In some boroughs the common councils seem to have been formed out of fragments of the leet juries, whilst in others we have reason to suppose that they were what their name strictly imports, councillors, called into the chamber by the alderman or presiding functionary with whom they were to advise. We have not discovered that there was any general principle in the mode of forming the constituency of the boroughs, nor can we assume that any one system of policy or common law right prevailed at any period throughout the realm. As far as we can judge, neither the opinion of those who treat every extension of authority beyond the select body as a popular usurpation, nor of those who view every municipal corporation as formed out of a symmetrical and uniform organisation of the people, can be supported. It is sufficient that we are enabled to collect the main principles of administration, namely, that the municipal magistracy and municipal councils were the resident and effective heads of the community, and that the community probably included in its members all who shared in its burthens and were liable to fill its offices."[1]

Thirdly, we have noted that municipal institutions seem to have been considered as entirely unconnected with other local institutions, as something so abnormal that their history could only be obtained from a study of their peculiar forms and ceremonies, rights and duties, practices and pretensions. But in one important particular it is now known that municipal institutions, at all events in England, Scotland, and Ireland,

---

[1] *Report of the Commissioners on Municipal Corporations*, i, p. 16.

have a feature common not only to the local institutions of England, but to other local institutions in all the Aryan lands. This is in the matter of land-holding. In spite of chartered rights, it is found that the land-rights of municipal corporations are parallel to the land-rights of village communities ; and the argument comes home to us that this fact links municipal with village institutions. The details of these archaic land-rights I have worked out in *Archæologia* (vol. xlvi, pp. 403-422), but the general position is worth considering here.

The old village communities have long ago been broken up, and their privileges, customs, and rights divided between the lord, the manor court, and the township court. They could not stand against the forces which swept over them when the Saxon kingdom began to rear its head as a European nationality, and, later on, when the Norman rule brought down upon them the usurping predispositions of a strong centralised and centralising monarchy. Therefore, as seen by the historian of to-day, these old village communities present but a scattered and mosaic-like picture. But, if anywhere, there should remain a more perfect organisation and a more perfect record of the process of change and development in those towns which from various circumstances early claimed the right of incorporation and protection from outside influences. Of course, there is a later disturbing element in this group of towns. Corporate towns, as a rule, obtained their local independence and power because they were rich enough to offer some price for such favours, or some resistance to oppression. These riches were obtained not from agriculture, the basis of the primitive village system, but from commerce, the most active opponent of the primitive village system. Therefore, we should expect to find that the result of commercial enterprise and success is the uprooting of old village institutions and the replacing by other institutions ; we should expect to come upon a period in the history of municipalities when they left off culti-

vating their own lands and began to collect
rents ; when they left off allotting to their
members plots in the municipal lands, and
began to appropriate to individual ownership that which once knew only common
ownership. But, though the aspect of the
archaic village community, viewed from
the evidence of municipal towns, may be
just as far off the primitive type as the
aspect viewed from the evidence of agricultural customs, the lines of change are more
marked, and we can work backwards upon
these lines. Considered, therefore, from
the general outlook of the subject, so far as
evidence has come down to us, the municipal towns contain better means of tracing
out the primitive village settlement of England than any other localities. The cor-
rectness of this assertion I have proved by
long-continued studies on the subject, and
these allow me to suggest that the land-
rights of municipal boroughs are archaic
land-rights, and that they can be identified
with ease with the land-rights of primitive
village communities.

When we pause, therefore, to ask what place municipal institutions have in English polity, we soon become aware that they enter early into the process of the building up of the nation ; that, side by side with village institutions, they have their place in the science of comparative politics; and that their history is not begun by a study of the *lex provinciæ* of Rome, and completed when we have considered how the Roman constitution would have developed during a thousand years of existence on English soil. In point of fact, it is just at this pause that we can fully grasp what an enquiry into the history of municipal corporations really means to the historical enquirer.   It means the ascertainment of whether modern municipal institutions are, on the whole, descendants from the Roman *lex provinciæ* or from Teutonic village settlements.   There must be many points in such an enquiry of extreme uncertainty and complexity.   Questions must arise as to whether this or that part of the municipal system is Roman, as derived from the later influences of Roman

law, or is Roman as derived from the earliest
and direct influences of Roman law. Questions must arise, too, as to whether this or
that particular municipal custom is derived
from a primitive village original or from a
derivative or borrowed custom existing elsewhere in its primitive form. But when all
these variations are considered, there must
remain the broad statement of the case—are
certain groups of municipal customs now
existing, or once existing, in England, the
result of Roman law developed on English
ground, or results of primitive institutions
developed alongside of other similarly placed
institutions? Between the Roman municipal organisation and the English village
community there was just the similarity
that exists between an old man just totter-
ing to his grave and a new-born infant just
entering into life. Both sprang from a
common original ; the one had worked itself out, the other had not begun its development. Roman municipal institutions had
developed from the Latin village community, but through long years of change

and influences which had almost obliterated the original. There can be no question, therefore, as to what origin we are to ascribe municipal institutions in England ; they will bear the unquestionable stamp of their Roman original, or they will be so primitive as to be recognised at once as belonging to the village system.

The constitution of the municipal assembly in the various boroughs of England illustrates this proposition in a very interesting manner, and I will venture to touch upon the subject a little more closely.

If we turn, in the first place, to London, we can discover certain idiosyncracies which proclaim the existence of facts not to be met with elsewhere. Nothing is more curious than the history of the London folkmoot. We see it standing out, now and again, in all its original strength, attended by all the citizens in early Teutonic fashion ; but we see towering behind it, overshadowing it too, a small, compact body of aldermen, just such a body, in fact, as Mr. Coote tells us governed the

Roman municipia, a high class of citizens —optimates, meliores, primates, potentes —who monopolised all municipal power and privilege, to the absolute exclusion of the other class.[1] The folkmoot was held in the open air, upon a piece of ground at the east end of St. Paul's Church, adjoining the Cross.[2] Here, at all events, we stand upon undoubted Teutonic ground, conquered from the Roman by men who knew and loved the village institutions they sought to transplant into the city. But then there is no evidence that this assembly of the citizens ever wholly dominated the city, and was recognised as the supreme council ; but it seems more than probable, since at times it took its part in those survivals of the old primary assemblies of the nation which met to elect their king.[3]

[1] *Romans in Britain*, p. 368.
[2] See *Liber Custumarum*, pp. 338, 339, and my *Primitive Folkmoots*, p. 158, where I have discussed the archaic importance of this.
[3] For the significance of the action of the London folkmoot in the election of Stephen, see Green's *History of the English People*, vol. i, pp. 151-152 ; Freeman's *Norman Conquest*, vol. v, pp. 245, 305. That

The fight between the popular assembly, or folkmoot, where every citizen had a right to attend, and the smaller body, is well related in the *Chronicles of the Mayor and Sheriffs of London,* 1188 to 1274. In 1249, upon the Abbot of Westminster and his advisers desiring to hold a conference with the mayor and aldermen, " the whole of the populace opposed it, and would not allow them, without the whole of the commons being present, to treat at all of the matter" (p. 18). Again, in 1257, on the occasion of charges being made against certain aldermen, the King gave orders to the sheriffs to convene the folkmoot on the morrow at Saint Paul's Cross, upon which day all the aldermen and citizens came there. The proceedings are fully described, but the passage interesting to us is the following: " To which inquiry (no conference being first held among the discreet men of

this connection of the London folkmoot was kept up is shown by the oath of fealty the citizens in assembly gave to Prince Edward, 1252. See *Chronicles of the Mayors and Sheriffs of London,* p. 20.

the city, as is usually the practice) answer
was made by some of the populace, sons of
divers mothers, many of them born without
the city, and many of servile condition,
with loud shouts of 'Nay, nay, nay'" (p.
38). In 1262 we have the following remarkable passage. The mayor, Thomas
FitzThomas, during the time of his mayor-
alty, had so pampered the city populace,
that, styling themselves the "commons of
the city", they had obtained the first voice
in the city. For the mayor, in doing all
that he had to do, acted and determined
through them, and would say to them, "Is
it your will that so it shall be?" and then
if they answered "Ya, ya", so it was done.
And on the other hand, the aldermen or
chief citizens were little or not at all consulted on such matters (p. 59). In 1265 the
populace cried "Nay, nay" to the proposed
election of William FitzRichard as sheriff,
and demanded Thomas FitzThomas (p. 91).
In 1266 "the low people arose, calling
themselves the commons of the city" (p.
95). In 1271 the old dispute broke out

again in the election of mayor, and the record of this is very instructive (pp. 154-156).

In these curious and instructive passages I cannot doubt that we have a record of the final chapters of the history of the Teutonic folkmoot in London. Its name, its place of meeting, its popular form, its formula of "Yea, yea", or "Nay, nay",[1] all proclaim its primitive origin. But then under what circumstances do we see it with these evident signs of its historical origin ? There are by its side " the discreet men of the city". We never meet with it, either before the date of these records we have quoted or afterwards, as the dominant power of the city, impressing its forms and ceremonies, its political system, its derivative forces, upon the municipal history of the city. It was never powerful; it was only fitful. And we may well ask why the Teutonic conqueror who met in his folkmoot, without let or hindrance, bowed in municipal government to another body,

[1] Cf. Freeman's *Comparative Politics*, sect. 5.

separate and distinct from it? The answer I am inclined to seek in the masterful pages of Mr. Coote's *Romans in Britain*, where I find that Roman prowess, ingenuity, commercial acumen, and political insight, managed to keep at bay in some places the savage barbarism of Teutonic conquest.

The position of the assembly in the boroughs of England may best be gathered from the first report of the Municipal Corporation Commissioners of 1835. They say, " Without inquiring when corporations in this country assumed their present form, it may be safely asserted that the body, however named, which was originally intended to share in the rights which the early charters conferred, embraced the great mass of the householders or inhabitants. By degrees, exclusive qualifications were insisted on with increasing strictness and with new exceptions, as the privileges to which these exclusive bodies laid claim rose in importance."[1]

[1] *Report of Commissioners on Municipal Corporations*, vol. i, p. 20.

This is official language, not historical ; but it carries, nevertheless, an important signification when compared with other facts taken from the same source.

"The most common and most striking defect in the municipal corporations of England and Wales is, that the corporate bodies exist independently of the communities among which they are formed. The corporations look upon themselves, and are considered by the inhabitants, as separate and exclusive bodies ; they have powers and privileges within the towns and cities from which they are named, but in most places all identity of interest between the corporation and the inhabitants has disappeared. This is the case even when the corporation includes a large body of inhabitant freemen ; it appears in a more striking degree, as the powers of the corporation have been restricted to smaller numbers of the resident population ; and still more glaringly, when the local privileges have been conferred on non-resident freemen, to the exclusion of the inhabitants to whom they rightly ought to belong."[1]

Guided by what is known about the London assembly this is very interesting, and the popular general assembly is fully shown to have been a part of mediæval and later English municipal constitutions by the strong evidence of its existence which was placed before the Commissioners of 1835. They are able to report as follows : " A distinction of great practical importance may be made between corporations consisting of a definite and those of an indefinite number. Most of the charters incorporate the men and inhabitants of the borough. There are very few charters which unequivocally designate the corporate body as a small and definite number of persons, but in many places, custom (supported by the silence of the charters as to any general right to the franchise, and by its disuse and oblivion, where any such may have formerly existed) has practically established the same restricted constitution. A very numerous

---

[1] *Mun. Corp. Com.*, vol. i, p. 32.

class of corporations exists, which may be considered as occupying a middle place between those in which the number of corporators is indefinite, and those in which it is now treated as necessarily definite. This class consists of the corporations in which, although there is no doubt, both from the wording of the charters, and from the modern practice, that the number of corporators may be indefinite, it has been the policy of the ruling body to restrict the number, so as to retain all the privileges constitutionally belonging to a large and indefinite body in the hands of a small and select one.

"In a great proportion of the instances in which the number of corporators is, both in constitution and fact, large and indefinite, the freemen have no share in the management of the affairs of the corporation : this prevails to so great an extent that, in such corporations, the Commissioners often found that the freemen had long ceased to consider themselves as forming any part of the corporation, which term, in popular language, was exclusively applied to the ruling body. In some places this notion has been further refined upon, and a distinction has been drawn in the large indefinite body of corporators, between those elected by the ruling body, and those claiming by an independent right, the former class only being treated as forming an integral part of the corporation."[1]

And a little later on they say: "The share which the freemen at large now take in the election of their governing bodies and corporate officers, is in most places very limited.

"In a great majority of those towns in which there is a large body of freemen, they have no share whatever in those elections. In a few instances, such as Berwick-upon-Tweed, Ipswich, and Carmarthen, they have the right of electing, from among themselves, all, or nearly all, the corporate officers; in others, such as Beverley and Pontefract, they elect only the mayor; in

[1] *Report of Commissioners on Municipal Corporations,* vol. i, p. 18.

Norwich, they elect the aldermen, common councilmen, and one of the two sheriffs ; in some, such as Plymouth, they have the right of electing their officers out of a select body ; in others, as Oxford and Swansea, they have only the power of selection of the nominees of such a select body. In many places, where the system of self-election now prevails, no trace exists of a more popular mode having been used at any time ; in others, such as Newcastle-under-Lyme and Bridgnorth, the right appears clearly to have been taken away from the freemen by the ancient usurpation of the select body ; and in the case of Newcastle-under-Lyme it has been recently restored, after an interval of two hundred years, by a decision of the Court of King's Bench.

"In some towns these rights are possessed only by the resident freemen ; in other places by all the freemen, whether resident or non-resident. The latter is the more common case."[1]

[1] *Mun. Corp. Com.*, vol. i, p. 20.

From these interesting passages it is clear that much might be gained by a more minute study of municipal antiquities than has yet been given. For the present, the general conclusions of the Commissioners must be accepted as evidence of the proposition I would advance, that municipal institutions are based upon Teutonic principles of government rather than Roman, except in some few cases like London, where special influences have been at work to favour a continuity from Roman times.

Municipal archives, like other national documents, have been treated with scant attention during the past. Mr. Halliwell-Phillipps, reporting to the British Archæological Association on the municipal archives of Dorset, found that a large part of the town papers of Weymouth were in private hands, being only thus saved from the waste-paper basket;[1] and we learn from

---

[1] It is, I think, worth quoting Mr. Halliwell-Phillipps's words in full here: "At Weymouth I find that a large part of the town papers are in private hands, belonging to Mr. Sherren, who acquired them at the time when the Municipal Reform Act, amongst

the Historical Manuscripts Commission that Mr. James Sherren had rescued them from a stable, where they had been deposited to await the tender mercies of the housemaid and fire-grate (*5th Report*, p. 576). On August 1st, 1879, these valuable documents were offered for sale by auction, and fortunately the Corporation has again become possessed of these national memorials. We may be spared the fear of such possible vandalism in the future, it is hoped, and certainly the labours of the Historical Manuscripts Commission will greatly help us herein.

But all danger is not yet passed. In the *Antiquary* for August 1885, we learn a very terrible state of things relative to the regalia of Exeter :—"The careless manner in which the most valuable portion of it is preserved at the Guildhall is open to the other evils, led to the ousting of what in many places was deemed dusty rubbish. It is fortunate that Mr. Sherren intervened to save from the waste-paper basket, by purchase, a quantity of curious matter of great local interest."—"The Municipal Archives of Dorset", *British Archæological Association*, vol. xxviii, p. 28.

gravest objection. The priceless swords,—the only known examples of early royal swords existing in England to-day ; the maces, and other things appertaining thereto, are kept in a flimsy cupboard on the top of the stairs—a cupboard that any schoolboy could break open with a jack-knife. A window is close by, communicating with the roofs of adjacent houses, and through it any one, with even only ordinary address, could readily make off with the whole paraphernalia, without the inspector and the police in their offices beneath being any the wiser. Further, if the thief took the trouble to fasten the cupboard doors again after him, the loss would, in all probability, not be discovered until the next time the insignia were wanted."

After the passing of the Municipal Reform Act of 1835, much of the old corporation archives were entirely destroyed. Instances of this are given in the *Gentleman's Magazine* and other contemporary authorities. In the above-mentioned journal for March 1836 the following facts are recorded:

"The new Corporations have, in some places, made a perfect clearance of the insignia of office and other property of their predecessors. At Leicester everything of the kind has been sold off. An ancient tobacco-box, of a very curious pattern, chased with the town arms upon the lid, with the name of the donor inscribed beneath, and the date of 1682, weight 8 oz. 13 dwts., was sold after the rate of 27s. per ounce. The first civic mace weighed 5 oz. 4 dwts., and was sold for £9 ; the second, 5 oz. 8 dwts., was sold for £6 15s. ; the third, 5 oz. 10 dwts., was sold for £6 6s. ; the recorder's mace, 36 oz., was sold for £16 ; the fifth was the large, grand state mace, richly chased and gilt. It weighed upwards of 100 ounces, and was in an excellent state of preservation, and realised the sum of £85. Besides these there was a fine portrait of the late William Pitt, presented to the Corporation by Samuel Smith, Esq., a late Member for the borough, which sold for fifty guineas.

"At Hull a motion was made that the

regalia, viz., the sword of state, the mace, and cap of maintenance, should be deposited in the Museum of the Philosophical Society, as objects of antiquarian interest and curiosity; but this proposal creating a fear that such a display of the 'baubles' would place them too highly in the estimation of the people, a radical councillor, who asserted, that 'he would rather lock them up in a dark room, and throw the key into the Humber', moved, as an amendment, that they should remain in the custody of the mayor for the time being, and this amendment was carried by a majority of 17 to 4. The sword was presented to the town by Henry VIII in 1541."

A better spirit is happily now prevalent, for when, on Oct. 5th, 1885, the annual convocation, or court, of the mayor, burgesses, and capital inhabitants of Marazion met together, in accordance with old custom, to elect "one fit and sufficient person" to serve the office of mayor for the last time, the proceedings were characterised, at least, by decorum. It is about 290 years since the first Mayor of "Marghasiewe" was chosen. Under a recent Act of Parliament the borough loses its charter in March next. "Before eleven o'clock" in the forenoon the mayor, accompanied by the town-clerk, took their places in the council-chamber. In accordance with the ancient custom, the insignia of the corporation were placed on the table. In the centre of the table lay the charter. On either side of the charter were laid the maces. These are of silver, and date from 1768. They have the town arms (three castellated towers embossed on the coronæ), and also the inscription, "Purchased by the Corporation of Marazion: Humphrey Coles, mayor, 1768." On the second department of their shafts are engraved the names of the eight burgesses and nine capital inhabitants. The length of the maces is 3 feet 1 inch each, and their weight 67 ounces 2 pennyweights each. The mayor's staff of office (a walking-stick) bears the date of 1684. On the top of the silver-mounted head, within a circle surrounding the town arms, is a Latin inscription. There is also the inscription, " Francis St. Aubyn, armiger, mayor of this corporation in 1694." The seals, too, lay in their proper place: the one cut in ivory, and the other sunk in copper, plated, are 1¾ inches in diameter, and have inscribed in a circle surrounding the town arms, " Sigill. maioris ville et borou de Marghasion." On the table also lay a copy of the notice convening the meeting, drawn up in accordance with ancient usage, and printed, as deemed appropriate for this occasion, on black-edged note-paper. The question as to whether some steps should not be taken with a view to keeping the charter, muniments, papers, and maces of the corporation in the borough was discussed, and a deputation waited on the Charity Commissioners with a request to keep the municipal insignia in the borough.

Turning now to the bibliography of our subject, it will be found that on the general history of municipal institutions the following are the most important authorities :—

First Report of the Commissioners appointed to inquire into the Municipal Corporations in

England and Wales. Ordered, by the House of Commons, to be printed, 30th March 1835. Folio, pp. 131.

Municipal Corporation (England and Wales). Appendix to the First Report of the Commissioners. Part i. Midland, Western, and South-Western Circuits. Pp. 1-662. Part ii. South-Eastern and Southern Circuits. Pp. 663-1408. Part iii. Northern and North-Midland Circuits. Pp. 1409-2080. Part iv. Eastern and North-Western Circuits. Pp. 2081-(2509-12*)-2940.

Analytical Index to the Reports of the Commissioners appointed to inquire into the Municipal Corporations of England and Wales. 1839. Folio.

Second Report of the Commissioners appointed to inquire into the Municipal Corporations in England and Wales (London and Southwark, London Companies). 1837. Folio.

Report of the Commissioners appointed to report and advise upon the Boundaries and Wards of certain Boroughs and Corporate Towns in England and Wales. Part i. Aberystwith to Faversham. Part ii. Folkestone to Nottingham. Part iii. Oswestry to York, 1837. Folio.

Municipal Corporations (Ireland) : General Report of the Commissioners, 1835. Folio.

Municipal Corporations (Scotland) : General Report of the Commissioners appointed to

inquire into the state of Municipal Corporations in Scotland, 1835.   Folio, pp. 99.
Appendix to the General Report of the Commissioners, 1835.   Folio, pp. 101.
Local Reports of the Commissioners, 1835-
1836.   Three parts, fol., pp. 463, 441, 192.

The importance of these reports can
scarcely be overrated, though the historian
must ever lament that the commissioners
did not extend their enquiries into the customs and local rights and privileges outside
the charter.

It is not often that the reports of a parliamentary commission can be of so much
service to the cause of history as those which
deal with the condition of the municipal
corporations of Great Britain.   Standing
as they do between the old and the new,
as the record of institutions which have to
a great extent been self-developed and not
created by legislation, they concentrate
within, their pages a mass of information
which, in the absence of local histories, is of
great value.   But, unhappily, this information is neither exhaustive nor so critically
accurate as the historian must require.   The

pages bear unmistakable signs of hasty and purely official work, and one has to lament that the protests of Sir Francis Palgrave and Mr. Hogg should be so well founded. Appreciating to the full what is to be found in the six thousand pages devoted to the subject, there is great room still for the well-founded regrets for what has not been recorded, and is perhaps now irretrievably lost. Still it is only necessary to contemplate for one moment the progress of municipal history in England to understand the position that these Reports occupy as the most valuable record of a very important epoch. We see groups of towns rising into prominent importance, new groups springing into existence, other groups beginning to decay. But to understand the full significance of this factor in English municipal history, a synthetical arrangement at one definite period of the recorded institutions of towns making up these several groups is positively necessary; and it is in this position of importance that I would place the Reports of the Commissioners of 1835, notwithstanding the lamentable defects in the information supplied, already alluded to. We learn thereby to appreciate and understand the position occupied by such towns as London, Manchester, Leeds, Liverpool, and others, as types of the fullest development of municipal institutions; we learn to class in groups such towns as Maidstone, Norwich, Oxford, Hull, and others, where local vigour has given way to corruption, and where some of the most historical rights and privileges have been swept away; we gather from such groups as Nottingham, Malmesbury, Berwick-on-Tweed, Chippenham, Marlborough, Arundel, and others, that many of our municipal institutions had a previous existence as township, or even village, institutions; and lastly, groups consisting of Aberystwith, Cardigan, and most of the Welsh boroughs, and a few English, such as Altrincham, Dursley, Romford, Wootton-under-Edge, show us that the old manorial privileges have also entered into the construction of English municipal history.

Information thus arranged from materials collected within the space of two years, and therefore belonging to the same period, enables the scientific historian to study the question from that comparative point of view which is the basis of all modern research, and enables the student of municipal institutions to demonstrate what the constitutional historian asserts must be the case, only under forms which he is scarcely able to identify, and which lie outside his scope and period, namely, that relics of the older system survive in the modern corporations.[1]

The other authorities on general municipal history and archives are varied and numerous. Particularly should be noted Mr. Fletcher's very admirable analysis of the Reports of the Commissioners of 1835, printed in the *Journal of the Statistical Society*, vol. v. Many articles occur in the fugitive literature of the day, and in the *Transactions* of the local archæological societies, the most important of which are duly noticed in the following pages. Some

[1] See Stubbs's *Const. Hist.*, vol. i, p. 424.

interesting articles appear occasionally in local newspapers, the *Leeds Mercury* particularly giving, during its issues for the year 1884, many curious papers on the seals and arms of the corporations of England. The following list is believed to contain the principal authorities, however:—

Amyot (Thomas), Remarks on the Population of English Cities in the Time of Edward the Third. *Archæologia*, vol. xx, pp. 524-531.

Arnold (Thomas James), A Treatise on the Law relating to Municipal Corporations in England and Wales. Second edition, with chapters on Practice by Samuel George Johnston. London, 1875. 8vo, pp. xxxviii, 250. Appendix, pp. ccxcix, and Index. [First edition (without chapters on Practice). London, 1851. 8vo, pp. xxiv, 256 ; appendix, cclxxxviii; and index.]

Astle (Thomas), Account of the Seals of the King's Royal Boroughs and Magnates of Scotland. London, 1792. Fol.

Brady (Robert), An Historical Treatise of Cities and Burghs or Boroughs, showing their original, and whence and from whom they received their liberties, privileges, and immunities ; what they were, and what made and constituted a Free Burgh and Free Burgesses. As also showing when they first sent their

H

representatives to Parliament. With a concurrent discourse of most matters and things incident or relating thereto. London, 1690. Folio, pp. vi, 91; insertions, 2 pp.; appendix, pp. 41.

The same. Second edition. London, 1704. Folio, pp. as before. [The same book with a new title-page, a mistake in the pagination being repeated, pp. 84, 25, 26, 89, 90, 91, 88, then commencing with appendix, pp. 1-41.]

—— A new edition, corrected. London, 1777. Pp. iv, 170; appendix, 55; index.

Chamberlain (Right Hon. J.), Municipal Public Houses. *Fortnightly Review*, 1877, vol. xxi, pp. 147-159. [Diagram facing p. 148.]

Cockburn (A. E.), The Corporations of England and Wales : an account of the constitution, privileges, powers, revenues, and expenditure of each corporation, collected from the *Reports of the Commissioners.* London, 1835. 2 vols., 8vo.

Cornhill Magazine, Unreformed Corporations, July 1880, pp. 77-85.

Cripps (Wilfred Joseph), College and Corporation Plate (South Kensington Museum Art Handbooks). London, 1881. 8vo, pp. xii, 155. [This book does not devote more attention to the artistic than the historical plate.]

Documents connected with the Question of Reform in the Royal Burghs of Scotland.

Second edition. Edinburgh, 1819. 8vo, pp. viii, 144. The Preface is signed "A. B."

Fletcher (Joseph), Statistics of the Municipal Institutions of the English Towns. *Journ. Statistical Society of London*, 1842, v, 97-168.

General Report to the King in Council from the Honourable Board of Commissioners on the Public Records. Vol. xv, large folio, 1837.

Contains Reports upon the Records of the following boroughs :—Altrincham, Andover, Ashburton, Axbridge, Banbury, Basingstoke, Beccles, Beverley, Bishops Castle, Bodmin, Bradninch, Bridgenorth, Bridgewater, Bridport, Burford, Callington, Cardiff, Cardigan, Carlisle, Carnarvon, Chard, Chesterfield, Chippenham, Christchurch, Cirencester, Cockermouth, Colnbrook, Cowbridge, Cricklade, Crowcombe, Dartmouth, Deal, Devizes, Dover, Dudley, Dunmow, Dunwich, Durham, Falmouth, Farnham, Folkestone, Garstang, Glastonbury, Godalming, Grampound, Grantham, Greenwich, Grinstead, Guildford, Harwich, Hastings, Hemel Hempstead, Hereford, Holt, Honiton, Horsham, Huntington, Hythe, Knaresborough, Lampeter, Langport, Llanidloes, Leeds, Leominster, Lydford, Lincoln, Liskeard, London, Looe (East), Looe (West), Longhor, Louth, Lyme, Maidenhead, Maldon, Marazion, Monmouth, Morpeth, Newcastle-under-Lyme, Newport, Newton, Oswestry, Penryn, Plymouth, Pontefract, Portsmouth, Preston, Queensboro', Radnor, Reigate, Ret-ford (East), Saffron Walden, St. Germains, Salisbury, Sandwich, Scarborough, Southampton, Southwold, Tenterden, Thornbury, Tiverton, Totnes, Tregony, Usk, Wareham, Warwick, Watchet, Wenlock, Weobly, Westbury, Weymouth, Wisbech, Wokingham, Woodstock, Worcester, Wycombe, Yarmouth. Pp. 428-512.

Gentleman's Magazine, Reflections on the Constitution of Incorporated Boroughs. 1787 (1), pp. 9-10, 105-107, 953-954.

Gilbert (J. T.), Historic and Municipal Documents of Ireland, A.D. 1172-1420, from the Archives of the City of Dublin, etc. London [Record Publications], 1870. 8vo, pp. lxxxviii, 560.

Gomme (George Laurence), Index of Municipal Offices ; compiled from the appendices to the first Report of the Commissioners appointed to inquire into the municipal corporations in England and Wales, 1835 ; with an Historical Introduction. London, published for the Index Society, 1879. 4to, pp. 77.

———— On Traces of the Primitive Village Community in English Municipal Institutions. *Archaeologia*, 1881, vol. xlvi, pp. 403-422.

Graves (Rev. James), The Records of the Ancient Borough-Towns of the County of Kilkenny. *Kilkenny Arch. Soc.*, vol. i (N.S.), pp. 84-93.

Gross (Dr. Charles), The Affiliation of Mediæval Boroughs. *Antiquary* (1885), vol. xi,
pp. 142-147, 199-203, 233-239.

Halliwell-Phillipps (J. O.), The Municipal
Archives of Dorset. *Journ. Arch. Assoc.*,
xxviii, 28-31.

Irving (Joseph), On the Origin and Influences
of Burghs in Scotland. *Trans. Glasgow
Arch. Soc.*, i, pp. 333-353.

Lambert (George), Civic and other Maces.
Antiquary, vol. i, pp. 66-70.

Madox (Thomas), Firma Burgi; or, an Historical Essay concerning the Cities, Towns,
and Boroughs of England, taken from the
Records. London, 1726. Folio, 11 leaves,
pp. 297 and index.

Merewether (Henry Alworth) and Archibald
John Stephens, The History of the Boroughs
and Municipal Corporations of the United
Kingdom, from the earliest to the present
time : with an examination of Records, Charters, and other documents illustrative of their
constitution and powers. London, 1835. 3
vols. 8vo, pp. lxxi, 16 pages of tables, 577 ;
577 (*sic*) - 1469 ; 1469 (*sic*) - 2413. [Arranged
under British Period, Roman Period, Saxon
Period, and from thence under each reign,
ending with William IV.]

Oldfield (T. H. B.), An Entire and Complete
History, political and personal, of the
Boroughs of Great Britain, together with the

Cinque Ports, to which is prefixed an original sketch of constitutional rights. London, 1792. 2 vols. 8vo. [Treats of the boroughs under the headings : (1) Political Character ; (2) Ancient State and Representation ; (3) Corporation ; (4) Right of Election ; (5) Number of Voters ; (6) Returning Officers ; (7) Patron.]

The same. Second edition, corrected and improved [the sketch of constitutional rights is not included]. London, 1794-97. 2 vols. 8vo, pp. ix, 434 ; 484.

The same. New edition, corrected [with author's name]. London, no date. 3 vols. 8vo, pp. xxii, 434 ; viii, 484 ; 548.

Palgrave (Sir Francis), Observations on the principles to be adopted in the establishment of New Municipal Corporations, together with the heads of a bill for their future regulation and government. London, 1832. 8vo, pp. xlvi, 71.

Parliamentary Publications. Returns from those boroughs, cities, etc., which may elect officers on a Sunday, together with the regulations in such a case. 1833 (4).

Payne (William), A Treatise on Municipal Rights, commencing with a summary account of the origin and progress of Society and Government, and comprising a concise view of the state thereof, from the earliest period of British history to the institution of Corporations in general and that of the City of London in particular, with an account of the ancient modes of electing the Mayors and Sheriffs of London, and the Representatives in Parliament, and various other matters relating to the Court of Common Council and the Livery, connected with the public rights of the Citizens of London, and applicable to the present state of the times. London, 1813. 8vo, pp. xiv, 144.

Picton (J. A.), Self-Government in Towns. *Contemporary Review,* 1878, vol. xxxiv, pp. 678-699.

Reports of the Royal Commission on Historical Manuscripts. Presented to both Houses of Parliament by command of Her Majesty. London, 1874-1881. 8 vols. folio.

Reports on the Records of the following boroughs are given, the Roman figures indicating the number of the report, and the Arabic the pages occupied by the report :—

Aberdeen, i, 121-123 ; Abingdon, i, 98-99, ii, 149-150; Axbridge, ii, 300-308; Berwick-on-Tweed, iii, 308-310 ; Bridgewater, i, 99, iii, 310-320 ; Bridport, vi, 475-499 ; Cambridge, i, 99-100 ; Chester, viii, 355-403; Cork, i, 128-129; Coventry, i, 100-102; Dartmouth, v, 597-606; Dublin, i, 129; Edinburgh, i, 126; Faversham, vi, 500-511 ; Folkestone, v, 590-592 ; Fordwich, v, 606-608; High Wycombe, v, 554-565 ; Hythe, iv, 429-439; Kilkenny, i, 129-131; Kingston-on-Thames, iii, 331-333 ; Kirkcud-

bright, iv, 538-539; Launceston, vi, 524-526 ;
Leicester, viii, 403-441; Limerick, i, 131; Lydd,
v, 516-533; Montrose, ii, 205-206; Morpeth, vi,
526-540; New Romney, iv, 439-442, v, 533-554,
vi, 540-545 ; Norwich, i, 102-104 ; Nottingham, i, 105-106 ; Perth, v, 655 ; Pontefract,
viii, 269-276 ; Rye, v, 488-516 ; St. Albans, v,
565-568 ; Sandwich, v, 568-571; Tenterden,
vi, 569-572 ; Totnes, iii, 341-350 ; Walling-
ford, vi, 572-594 ; Waterford, i, 131-132 ;
Wells, i, 106-108 ; Weymouth and Melcombe
Regis, v, 575-590 ; Winchester, vi, 605; York,
i, 108-110.

Scottish Burgh Records Society:[1] Ancient Laws
and Customs of the Burghs of Scotland.
Edinburgh, 1868.   4to, pp. l, 252.

Vol. i, A.D. 1124-1424.   i, Leges quatuor
Burgorum Edinburgh, Rokisburgh, Berewic,
Strivelin ; ii, Assise Regis Willelmi, the laws
of King William the Lion, in so far as these
relate to Burghs ; iii, Statuta Gilde ; iv, Regiam Maiestatem, certain laws concerning
burghs from the book of Regiam Maiestatem; v, Quoniam Attachiamenta, the laws
of the Barons in so far as concerns the
Burghs ; vi, Constitutiones noue pro Bur-
gensibus ; vii, Assisa de Tolloneis, of petty
customs called Toll ; viii, Custuma Por-
tuum, of the custom of Schippis ; ix, Articuli

[1] It should be noted that the British Museum
Library does not possess these exceedingly valuable
publications.

inquirendi in itinere camerarii, of inquiries in the Chalmerlan air ; x, Juramenta officiariorum ; xi, Iter Camerarii, the Chalmerlan air ; xii, Curia quatuor Burgorum, the court of the four burghs—Edinburgh, Stirling, Berwick, and Roxburgh ; xiii, Fragmenta Collecta; xiv, Acta Parliamentorum, regis David Secundi ; xv, Obligations of the Towns and Burgesses of Scotland anent the ransom of King David II.—Glossary and Index.

Scottish Burgh Records Society, Miscellany of the. Edinburgh, 1881. 4to, pp. ci, 295.

Containing : i, Report by Thomas Tucker upon the Settlement of the Revenues of Excise and Customs in Scotland, A.D. MDCLVI; ii, Register containing the State and Condition of every Burgh within the Kingdom of Scotland, in the year 1692 ; iii, Setts of the Royal Burghs of Scotland.

Smith (William), Old Yorkshire. London, 1881. 8vo. Vol. i, pp. 226-231 ; ii, 192-199, contain articles on Seals of the Yorkshire Corporations.

Stubbs (Dr. W.), Select Charters and other illustrations of English Constitutional History, from the earliest times to the reign of Edward the First. Oxford, 1870. 8vo, pp. xii, 530.

Contains the following charters: William I, charter to London ; Henry I, charters to London, Beverley, customs of Newcastle-upon-Tyne ; Henry II, charters of Winchester, Lincoln, and Nottingham ; Richard I, charters to Winchester and Lincoln ; John, charters to Nottingham, Northampton, Dunwich, Lincoln, York, Hartlepool, Niort, Helstone, London.

Thompson (James), An Essay on English Municipal History. London, 1867. 8vo, pp. xii, 196.

Contents : Cap. i, The Roman-British Municipalities ; ii, Saxon Town Institutions ; iii, The Borough of St. Albans ; iv-vii, The Borough of Leicester ; viii, The Borough of Preston ; ix-xi, The City of Norwich; xii, The Borough of Yarmouth ; xiii-xiv, On Market Towns not Incorporated ; xv, Municipal Insignia ; xvi, The French Communes ; xvii, Comparison between the French Communes and English Boroughs ; xviii, Practical Conclusions.

—— The Municipal Franchises of the Middle Ages, illustrated by documents from the archives of the town of Leicester. *Gentleman's Magazine*, 1851, vol. xxxv (N. S.), pp. 260-263, 596-599 ; vol. xxxvi (N. S.), pp. 244-249.

Vine (J. R. Somers), English Municipal Institutions : their growth and development from 1835 to 1879 statistically illustrated. London, 1879. 8vo, pp. viii, 272.

Contents: Introduction.—Nature and Constitution of the English Municipal Corporations.—Short Historical Sketch of the English

Municipalities.—Acts of Parliament relating to the English Municipal Corporations (1835-1878), with an outline of their general purport. —The Growth and Development of the English Municipalities subject to 5 and 6 Will. IV, c. 76, between 1835 and 1879.—The Unreformed Corporations. — Populous Districts not under Municipal Government.

Wilcock (J. W.), On Municipal Corporations. London, 1827. 8vo.

Worth (R. N.), The Ancient Boroughs of Cornwall, with notes on their arms and devices. *Journ. Arch. Assoc.*, xxxiii, pp. 179-190.

Wright (Thomas), On the Existence of Municipal Privileges under the Anglo-Saxons. *Archæologia*, vol. xxxii, 298-311.

Every municipal town has not yet found a historian, and those that have are not by any means satisfactory. A great deal of miscellaneous information may, however, be picked up from these local histories, though here, as in county histories, the same absence of information as to government and laws is to be noticed. Independently, however, of these local histories, much has been done with municipal archives, and the accompanying list of works on special boroughs is believed to be fairly complete.

Particular Boroughs.

Aberdeen :

Spalding Club. Extracts from the Council Register of the Burgh of Aberdeen, 1398-1625. Edited by John Stuart. 1844-48, 2 vols.

Scottish Burgh Records Society. Extracts from the Council Register of the Burgh of Aberdeen, 1625-1642. Edinburgh, 1871. 4to, pp. xxiv, 299.

The same, 1643-1747. Edinburgh, 1872. 4to, pp. lix, 392.

Axbridge :

Hunt (Rev. William), On the Charters and Municipal Government of Axbridge. *Somerset Arch. and Nat. Hist. Soc.*, xv, 6-20.

Bath :

Hunt (W.), The Early Royal Charters of Bath. *Somerset Arch. and Nat. Hist. Soc.*, xxii (1), 73-86.

Paynter (Vice-Admiral), Ancient Bath Charters. *Somerset Arch. and Nat. Hist. Soc.*, xxii (2), 1-9.

Falconer (R. W.), List of Charters connected with the City of Bath. Bath, 1858. 8vo.

King (Austin J.) and B. H. Watts, The Municipal Records of Bath, 1189 to 1604. Published with the approval of the Town Council and at the special request of the Bath Literary Society. London, 1885. 4to, pp. vii, 63, and appendix, pp. xliv.

Birmingham :

Bunce (John Thackray), History of the Corporation of Birmingham, with a sketch of the earlier history of the town. Published for the Corporation, 1878.

> Vol. i [only]. Contents : cap. i, Early Government of Birmingham ; ii, Gild of the Holy Cross ; iii, First Proposal of Incorporation ; iv, Birmingham in the Eighteenth Century ; v, Establishment of Street Commissioners— First regular Local Government ; vi, Petition for Charter of Incorporation ; vii, Opposition to Grant of Charter ; viii, Grant of the Charter ; ix, Election and Proceedings of the First Council ; x, The Birmingham Police Act ; xi, Validity of the Charter of Incorporation Disputed ; xii, The Charter enforced and confirmed ; xiii, Union of Governing Bodies in the Borough ; xiv, Summary and Review.

Bridgewater :

Odgers (J. Edwin), A Short Report on some MS. Accounts of the Commonalty of Bridgewater. *Somerset Arch. and Nat. Hist. Soc.*, xxiii, 38-48.

Brighton :

Borough of Brighton : Copies of the Deeds relating to the division of the tenantry lands in the parish of Brighthelmston in the year 1822, etc. Brighton, 1878. 8vo.

Bristol:

The City Charters, containing the original institution of Mayors, Recorders, Sheriffs, Town Clerks, and all other officers whatsoever. Bristol, 1736. 4to. [Another edition appeared in 1792.]

Cranidge (John), A Mirror for the Burgesses and Commonalty of that City of Bristol, in which is exhibited to their view a part of the great and many interesting benefactions and endowments of which the city hath to boast. Bristol, 1818. 8vo.

Bush (H), Bristol Town Duties : a collection of original and interesting documents intended to elucidate the above important subject. [n. d.]

Manchee (T. J.), The Bristol Charities : being the Report of the Commissioners for Enquiry concerning Charities in England and Wales, so far as relates to Charitable Institutions in Bristol. Bristol, 1831. 2 vols. 4to.

Nichols (J. F.), Notes on the Regalia of the Corporation of the City of Bristol. *Journ. Arch. Assoc.*, vol. xxxi, pp. 310-315.

Gutch (John Mathew), The present Mode of Election of the Mayor, Sheriffs, and Common Council of Bristol considered. Extracted from Felix Farley's *Bristol Journal*. Bristol, 1825. 8vo, pp. 50.

Planché (J. R.), On the Municipal Seals and Armorial Ensigns of the City of Bristol. *Journ. Arch. Assoc.*, xxxi, 180-189.

Ricart (R.), The Maire of Bristowe's Kalendar, 18 Edw. IV. Edited by Lucy Toulmin Smith. London (Camden Society), 1872, 4to.

Birch (W. de Gray), Original Documents relating to Bristol. London, 1874. 8vo.

Burton-on-Trent:

Ancient Charters relating to the Abbey and Town of Burton-on-Trent. (Original documents.) *Journ. Arch. Assoc.*, vii, 421-428.

Bury St. Edmunds:

Guildhall Feoffment Estates, as contained in the Decree of the 22nd July 1771. Bury St. Edmunds, 1772. 4to.

Canterbury:

Charters granted by Edward IV, Henry VII, James I, and Charles II, to the Citizens of Canterbury. Translated by a Citizen. Canterbury, 1791. 8vo.

Civis [pseud., *i.e.*, William Welfit], Minutes collected from the Ancient Records and Accounts in the Chamber of Canterbury, of Transactions in that City, from A.D. 1234. Canterbury, 1801-1802. Fol.

Brent (John), Canterbury in the Olden Times, from the municipal archives and other sources. Canterbury, 1860. 8vo.

The same. Second Edition. London, 1879. 8vo.

Wright (Thomas), Observations on the Municipal Archives of the City of Canterbury, with many extracts therefrom. 1844. 4to.

Chester :

The Case of the Citizens of Chester in answer to several petitions from Liverpool, Parkgate, and the Cheesemongers, and also to provide reasons against the Act to recover and preserve the navigation of the river Dee. Chester, 1735. Sh. fol.

Chesterfield :

Yeatman (Pym), Records of the Borough of Chesterfield, being a series of extracts from the archives of the Corporation of Chesterfield, and of other repositories. Chesterfield and Sheffield, 1884. 8vo, pp. xv, 172.

Chichester :

Street (Eugène E.), The Mayor and Corporation of St. Pancras, Chichester. *Suss. Arch. Coll.*, xxiv, 135-138.

Clare :

Armstead (J. B.), Some Account of the Court Leet of the Borough of Clare, with extracts from the verdicts of the Head Boroughs. *Suffolk Arch. Inst.*, ii, 103-112.

Clitheroe :

Harland (John), On some Charters and Grants

to the Borough of Clitheroe. (Original documents.) *Journ. Arch. Assoc.,* vi, 425-435.

Harland (John), Ancient Charters and other Muniments of the Borough of Clitheroe, in the county of Lancaster. From the original documents, with translations and notes. Manchester, 1851. 4to, pp. 52.

Clun :

A Concise Account of Ancient Documents relating to the Honour, Forest, and Borough of Clun in Shropshire, with copies of some of them, and Observations on Customs of Amobyr. Read to the meeting of the Archæological Institute at Shrewsbury, in August 1855. Shrewsbury, 1858. 4to.

Colchester :

Harrod (Henry), Calendar of the Court Rolls of the Borough of Colchester. Colchester, 1865. 4to.

—— Repertory of the Records and Evidence of the Borough of Colchester. Colchester, 1865. 4to.

—— Report on the Records of the Borough of Colchester, 1865. Colchester, 1865. 4to.

Round (J. Horace), The Domesday of Colchester. *Antiquary* (1882), vol. vi, pp. 5-9, 95-100, 251-256.

—— Municipal Offices : Colchester. *Antiquary* (1885), vol. xii, pp. 188-192 ; 240-245 ; vol. xiii, pp. 28-30.

I

Coventry :

Mayors, Bailiffs, and Sheriffs of Coventry.
Coventry, 1830. 12mo.

Dover:

Knocker (Edward), A Lecture on the Archives
of the Cinque Port and Borough of Dovor,
delivered before the corporation and inhabitants on the 25th day of April 1877 ; to which
is added a paper on the ancient connection
between the Cinque Ports and the borough of
Great Yarmouth. Dover, 1879. 8vo, pp. 117.

Dumbarton :

Scottish Burgh Records Society. Dumbarton
Burgh Records, 1627-1746. Dumbarton, 1870.
4to, pp. 107.

In the same volume are bound Dumbarton
Kirk-Sessions Records, pp. 9 ; Glasgow *v.*
Dumbarton, disputes regarding Clyde privileges, pp. 10 ; Provosts of the Burgh of Dumbarton, pp. 2 ; Members of Parliament for
Dumbarton county and burgh, 1608 to 1859,
pp. 3.

Dundee :

Maxwell (Alexander), The History of old
Dundee, narrated out of the Town Council
Register, with additions from contemporary
annals. Edinburgh and Dundee, 1884. 4to,
pp. 610.

Hay (William, Town Clerk), Collection of the
Charters, Writs, and Public Documents of

the Royal Burgh of Dundee, the Hospital, and Johnstone's Bequest, from 1292 to 1880. 1880. 4to. [Not printed for sale.]

Warden (Alex. I.), Burgh Laws of Dundee, with the History, Statutes, and the Proceedings of the Guild of Merchants and Fraternities of Craftsmen. London, 1872. 8vo, pp. x, 625.

Contents : Introduction — Burgh Laws of Dundee—Royal Acts and Statutes — The Guildry Incorporation of Dundee—The Nine Incorporated Trades of Dundee : Introduction, Historical Account, Proceedings of the Nine Trades, The Baker Trade, The Shoemaker Trade, The Glover Trade, The Tailor Trade, The Bonnet-maker Trade, The Flesher Trade, The Hammerman Trade, The Weaver Trade, The Dyer Trade—Pendicles of the Guildry—The Three United Trades : The Mason Trade, the Wright Trade, The Slater · Trade—The Maltmen Incorporation—Concluding Remarks—Glossary.

Dysart :

Euing (William), Notices from the Local Records of Dysart. Glasgow, 1853 (Maitland Club). 4to, pp. 72.

Muir (Rev. W.), Gleanings from the Records of Dysart, from 1545 to 1796. 4to, 1862.

Edinburgh :

City of Edinburgh : Rolls of Superiorities be.

longing to the Magistrates of the, from the
year 1567 to 1879. Drawn up, with Introductory Notice, by Robert Adam, City Chamberlain. 1877-80. 4 vols., large folio. [Not
printed for sale.]

Marwick (Jas. D.), History of the High Constables, with notes on the early watching,
cleaning, and other police arrangements of
the city of Edinburgh. Printed for private
circulation, 1865. Small 4to.

Scottish Burgh Records Society. Charters and
other Documents relating to the City of Edinburgh, A.D. 1143-1540. Edinburgh, 1871. 4to,
pp. xxvii, 281.

—— Extracts from the Records of the Burgh
of Edinburgh, A.D. 1403-1528. Edinburgh,
1869. 4to, pp. xxxvi, 339.

—— The same, A.D. 1528-1557. Edinburgh,
1871. 4to, pp. lvii, 369.

—— The same, A.D. 1557-1571. Edinburgh,
1875. 4to, pp. xxvii, 304.

Egremont:

Knowles (Rev. Canon), The Charters of the
Borough of Egremont. *Cumberland and
Westmoreland Antiquarian and Arch. Soc.,*
i, 282-287.

Exeter:

Antiquities of the City of Exeter : Giving an
account of the Laws and Customs of the
place, the Officers, Court of Judicature, Gates,

Walls, Rivers, Churches, and Privileges. Together with a Catalogue of all the Bishops,
Mayors, Sheriffs, from the year 1049 to 1677.
Collected by Richard Izacke, Esquire, Chamberlain thereof. 1681. 8vo.

Vowell [otherwise Hooker] (John), Orders enacted for Orphans, and for their Portions
within the Cities of Excester, with sundry
other instructions incident to the same. London, 1575. 4to.

—— A Pamphlet of the Officers, and Duties
of everie particular sworne officer of the Citie
of Excester. London, 1584. 4to.

Gidley (B. C.), On the Distinctive Style and
Title of the Corporation of the City of Exeter.
Exeter, 1875. 8vo.

Cotton (W.), and Venerable Archdeacon Henry
Woolcombe, Gleanings from the Municipal
and Cathedral Records relative to the history
of the City of Exeter. Exeter, 1877. 8vo, pp.
208, 38.

Wright (Thomas), The Municipal Archives of
Exeter. *Journ. Arch. Assoc.*, xviii, 306-317.

Fordwich :

Bryan (Benjamin), Some Account of the Ancient Borough of Fordwich, in Kent. *Reliquary*, 1877-8, vol. xviii, 65-70.

Glasgow :

Maitland Club : Burgh Records of the City of

Glasgow, MDLXXIII–MDLXXXI. Glasgow, 1832. 4to, pp. xxi, 160, illustrated. [The Prefatory Note is signed by John Smith.]

Maitland Club : Index to a private collection of Notices entituled Memorabilia of the City of Glasgow, selected from the Minute Books of the Burgh, MDLXXXVII–MDCCL. [Glasgow], 1836. 4to, pp. 20. [The "Notice" is signed by John Smith.]

Scottish Burgh Records Society. Extracts from the Records of the Burgh of Glasgow, A.D. 1573-1642. Glasgow, 1876. 4to, pp. lvi, 497.

MacGeorge (Andrew), An Inquiry as to the Armorial Insignia of the City of Glasgow. 1866. [Privately printed.]

Gloucester:

The State of the Case for the City of Gloucester against the Bill for Disuniting the two Hundreds of Dudstow and King's Barton from the said city. [London, 1680.] Fol.

Gowran:

Watters (Patrick), Documents connected with the Ancient Corporation for Gowran. *Hist. and Arch. Assoc. of Ireland*, vol. i, pt. ii, pp. 535-552.

Halifax:

Halifax and its Gibbet Law placed in a true light, together with a description of the town. London, 1708. 2 parts, 12mo.

Davis (J. W.), The Halifax Corporation. Vol. ii, pp. 205-210, of W. Smith's *Old Yorkshire.* London, 1881. 8vo.

Hastings :

Ross (Thomas), Hastings Documents. *Suss. Arch. Coll.*, xxiii, 85-118.

Cooper (W. D.), Notices of Hastings and its Municipal Institutions. Lewes, 1862. 8vo.

Hereford :

A Translation of the Charter granted to the City of Hereford by King William the Third . . . 1697. Hereford, 1820. 4to.

Johnson (Richard), A Lecture on the Ancient Customs of the City of Hereford. Hereford, 1845. 8vo.

Black (W. H.) and G. M. Hills, The Hereford Records and the Customs of Hereford. *Journal Arch. Assoc.*, xxvii, 453-488.

Johnson (Richard), The Ancient Customs of the City of Hereford, with translations of the earlier City Charters and Grants ; also some account of the Trades of the City, and other information relative to its early History. London and Hereford, 1868. 4to, pp. viii, 170.

Hull :

King (Kelburne), The Plate and Insignia of the Hull Corporation. Vol. i, pp. 231-236, of W. Smith's *Old Yorkshire.* London, 1881. 8vo.

Huntingdon :

Griffith (E.), Observations on a Collection of Ancient Records relative to the Borough of Huntingdon. 1827. 8vo.

Ipswich :

The principal Charters which have been granted the Corporation of Ipswich. Translated by R. Canning. London, 1754. 8vo.

Ancient and Modern Perambulations, and Extracts from Charters, Trials, and other Records relative to the Liberties of Ipswich, etc. Ipswich, 1815. 8vo.

Annalls (The) of Ipswiche. The lawes, customes, and govern^mt of the same, collected out of ye records, bookes, and writings of that town. By Nath^ll Bacon, serving as recorder and town clerk in that towne. Anno Dom. 1654. Edited by W. H. Richardson, M.A., with a Memoir by Sterling Westhorpe, Mayor of Ipswich, 1884-5. [Portrait of Bacon, from the original painting in the Town Hall, Ipswich.] Ipswich : printed for the subscribers by S. H. Cowell. 1884. 4to. [The above work, covering an important period of local history (1200-1648), has hitherto existed in MS. only, a sealed treasure in the archives of the town.]

Report by Committee on the various officers of the town of Ipswich, as originally constituted, and list of those proposed to be continued. Ipswich, 1838.

Kendal:

Nicholson (C.), History and Incidents connected with the Grants of the Three Royal Charters of Incorporation of the Borough of Kendal. London, 1875. 8vo.

Kilkenny:

Prim (Sir G. A.), The Corporation, Insignia, and olden Civic State of Kilkenny. *Hist. and Arch. Assoc. of Ireland*, vol. i, p. i, 280-305.

King's Lynn:

Harrod (Henry), Report on the Deeds and Records of the Borough of King's Lynn. King's Lynn, 1874. 4to.

Kingston-upon-Thames:

Roots (George), The Charters of the Town of Kingston-upon-Thames translated into English, with Occasional Notes. London, 1797. 8vo.

Kintore:

Watt (Alexander), The Early History of Kintore; with an account of the rights and privileges belonging to the heritors and community of the burgh; extracted from old records and charters. 8vo.

Leeds:

Smith (William), Old Yorkshire. London, 1881. 8vo. Vol. i, pp. 236-237, contains an article on the Leeds Civic Sceptre. Vol. ii, pp. 200-205, on the Records of Leeds.

Wardell (J.), Municipal History of Leeds. London, 1866. 8vo.

Leicester:

Kelly (William), The Great Mace, and other Corporation Insignia of the Borough of Leicester. Printed for private circulation. 1875. 8vo.

Leominster :

Townsend (G. F.), The Town and Borough of Leominster, with Illustrations of its ancient and modern History. Leominster, 1863. 8vo.

Lincoln :

Names of the Mayors, Bailiffs, Sheriffs, and Chamberlains of the City of Lincoln since 1313. Lincoln, 1787. 12mo.

Llantrissant :

Llantrissant Borough Charters. (Original Documents.) *Arch. Journ.*, xxix, 351-359.

London :

Briefe (A) Discourse, declaring and approving the necessarie and inviolable maintenance of the laudable customes of London. 1584. 12mo.

Analytical Index to the Series of Records known as the Remembrancia, preserved among the Archives of the City of London, A.D. 1579-1664. London, 1878. 8vo, pp. xviii, 623.

Antiquis (De) Legibus Liber: chronica maiorum et vicecomitum Londoniarum et quedam que contingebant temporibus illis ab anno

MCLXXVIII ad annum MCCLXXIV ; cum appen-
dice, nunc primum typis mandata, curante
Thoma Stapleton. (Camden Society), London, 1846. 4to, pp. cclxxii, 276.

Arnold's Chronicle, The Customs of London
otherwise called, containing, among divers
other matters, the original of the celebrated
poem of the " Nut Brown Maid". Reprinted
from the first edition, with the additions included in the second. London, 1811. 4to,
pp. lii, 300.

[The ballad is contained in pp. 193-203. A
reprint by Thomas Wright, F.S.A., of *The
Nut Brown Maid, from the earliest edition
of Arnold's Chronicle*, was issued in 1836.
London, sm. 4to, pp. xvi, 30.]

Ashton (John) and F. C. Price, Lord Mayors'
Shows in the Olden Time ; compiled from
various authentic drawings and ancient MSS.
showing the pageants and allegorical struc-
tures in the 15th and 16th centuries. London,
1883.

Bohun (W.), Privilegia Londini ; or the Rights,
Liberties, Privileges, Laws, and Customs of
the City of London. The third edition, with
large additions. London, 1723. 8vo, pp. xvi,
498, the Table.

The title-page bears the following contents:
1. The several charters granted to the said
City from King William I to the present
times. 2. The Magistrates and Officers there-

of, with their respective creations, elections, rights, duties, and authorities. 3. The Laws and Customs of the City as the same relate either to persons or estates of the Citizens— viz., of Freemen's Wills, Feme-Sole, Mer- chants, Orphans, Apprentices. etc. 4. The na- ture, jurisdiction, practice, and proceedings of the several Courts thereof, with tables of fees relating thereto. 5. The several statutes con- cerning the said City and Citizens alphabeti- cally digested. [First edition is dated 1702, and contains pp. 472 and Table.]

Brandon (Woodthorpe), The Customary Law of the City of London.   The distribution of the personal estates of Freemen dying intestate, etc.   London, 1845.   8vo, pp. 22.

—— An Inquiry into the Freedom of the City of London in connection with trade ; and into the laws and ordinances within the City respecting wholesale and retail traders and the power of the Corporation over per- sons carrying on trade within the City, not being free.   London, 1850.   8vo, pp. vi, 56.

—— A Treatise upon the Customary Law of Foreign Attachment, and the practice of the Mayor's Court of the City of London therein, with forms of procedure.   London, 1861. 8vo, pp. xix, 243.

—— Observations on County Courts and Lo- cal Municipal Courts as courts for the re- covery of small debts.   London, 1868.   8vo, pp. 31.

Brandon (Woodthorpe), The Lord Mayor's Court of the City of London, and the Customary Law of Foreign Attachment. London, 1876. 8vo, pp. xi, 71.

Brewer (Thomas), On the Guildhall of the City of London. *Journ. Arch. Assoc.*, viii, 83-94.

Carpenter (William), The Corporation of London, as it is, and as it should be. Comprising some account of the Legislative and Executive Bodies, the Incorporated Companies and Municipal Franchises ; of the income and expenditure of the Corporation and the management of its property ; of the past and present condition of the City Gaols ; and of the dispute between the Courts of Aldermen and Common Council. With an appendix comprising a list of all the Officers of the Corporation and of the Committees of Common Council, with an alphabetical list of the Members of the Court. London, 1847. 8vo, pp. iii, 112.

[Chancellor (William)], Some account of the several Wards, Precincts, and Parishes in the City of London, to which is added lists of the Lord Mayors, Sheriffs, and other Officers, from the year 1660 to the present time ; of the Court of Aldermen at the time of the Revolution in 1688 ; and of the Aldermen and Members of Parliament since that period. [London], 1772. 12mo, pp. 131.

City Liberties, or the Rights and Privileges of Freemen; being a concise abridgment of all the Laws, Charters, By-laws, and Customs of London down to this time ; containing the liberties and advantages of the Citizens, their wives, widows, orphans, and others, and the laws concerning Wills, administration and disbursement of Estates, Actions, Attachments, and Sequestrations ; also of binding forth Apprentices, taking out Freedoms, election of Officers and Courts in the City, Companies of Trade, etc., as regulated by late statutes. Very useful to all Citizens and other inhabitants of the City of London. In the Savoy, 1732. 8vo, pp. viii, 168, and Table of Heads.

Collier (J. Payne), An Account of a MS. of Thomas Norton relating to the Ancient Duties of the Lord Mayor and Corporation of London. *Archæologia*, vol. xxxvi, pp. 97-104.

[Colthrop (Sir Henry)], The Liberties, Usages, and Customs of the City of London, confirmed by especiall Acts of Parliament, with the time of their Confirmation ; also divers ample and most beneficiall Charters granted by King Henry the 6th, King Edward the 4th, King Henry the 7th, not confirmed by Parliament, as the other Charters were. And where to find every particular Grant and Confirmation at large. Published for the good and benefit of this Honourable City. London, 1674. Sm. 4to, pp. 25.

The same. London, printed by B. Alsop for Nicholas Vavasour, 1642. Sm. 4to, pp. 25.

Fairholt (F. W.), Collection of Lord Mayors' Pageants. London (Percy Society), 1843-1844. 2 vols., 8vo.

Firth (Joseph J. B.), Municipal London ; or, London Government as it is, and London under a Municipal Council. London, 1876. 8vo, pp. xvi, 775.

Caps. i to v, The Corporation of the City of London ; vi, The Metropolitan Board of Works ; vii, The London Vestries ; viii, The Gas Supply of London; ix, The Water Supply of London ; x and xi, Various Jurisdictions ; xii, Summary ; xiii, Corporation Reform ; xiv, Bills in Parliament ; xv, Methods of Reform discussed ; xvi to xxi, Constitution of the Supreme Council ; xxii and xxiii, Work of the Supreme Council ; xxiv, London in the Future. Index.

Fletcher (Joseph), A Statistical Account of the Ancient Prescriptive Jurisdictions over the Thames possessed by the Corporation of London. *Journ. Statistical Society of London*, 1841, iv, 99-110.

—— The Metropolis: its Boundaries, Extent, and Divisions for Local Government. *Journ. Statistical Society of London*, 1844, vol. vii, 103-143.

—— A Statistical Account of the Municipal Provisions for Paving, Lighting, and Cleaning the Streets and Public Places of the Metropolis, and for protecting them from Nuisances.

Journ. Statistical Society of London, 1846, ix, 204-222.

Fletcher (Joseph), Statistical Account of the Markets of London. *Journ. Statistical Society of London*, 1847, vol. x, 345-360.

Gilbert (William), The City: an Inquiry into the Corporation, its Livery Companies, and the administration of their Charities and Endowments. London, 1877. 8vo, pp. 376.

Gomme (George Laurence), On the Early Municipal History of London. *London and Middlesex Archæological Society.* 1885.

Harvey (Abraham), A Handbook to the Guildhall and the various Offices of the Corporation of London. London, 1862. 8vo, pp. 72.

Historical (The) Charters and Constitutional Documents of the City of London, with an Introduction and Notes by an Antiquary. London, 1884. 4to, pp. xlviii, 338.

Hobhouse (Sir Arthur), The Government of London. *Contemporary Review*, 1882, vol. xli, pp. 404-416.

Hughson (David), Multum in Parvo: The Privileges of Southwark, comprised in the Charters granted to the City of London by Edward III, Edward IV, Edward VI, and confirmed by Parliament, containing the whole of those charters and other authorities, to prove that Southwark and its inhabitants are under the sole jurisdiction of the City of

London and no other. Southwark 1817. 12mo, pp. 22.

Hughson (David), An Epitome of the Privileges of London, including Southwark, as granted by Royal Charters, confirmed by Acts of Parliament, and established by ancient custom; with remarks on the repeated invasions of the rights, franchises, and jurisdiction of the Metropolis of Great Britain. London, 1816. 12mo, pp. 287, and 7 leaves containing Introduction, Contents, and Glossary.

Hunt (Thomas), A Defence of the Charter and Municipal Rights of the City of London and the Rights of other Municipal Cities and Towns of England. Directed to the Citizens of London. London, printed by Richard Baldwin, no date. 4to, pp. 46.

Luffman (John), The Charters of London, complete; also Magna Charta, and the Bill of Rights. London, 1793. 8vo.

Mildmay (Sir William), The Method and Rule of Proceeding upon all Elections, Polls, and Scrutinies at Common Halls and Wardmotes within the City of London. The second edition. London, 1768. 8vo, pp. xii, 165 ; appendix, 24.

—— The same ; with additional notes on Wardmote Elections ; an historical review of the City Electoral Franchises ; and of the Incorporated Mysteries with their Liverymen, Electors of London, by Henry Kent S.

K

Causton. London, 1841. 8vo, pp. ccclxxxviii, 309.

Newall (W.), The Local Government of the Metropolis. *Contemporary Review*, 1873, vol. xxii, pp. 73-86.

———— The Municipality of London. *Contemporary Review*, 1875, vol. xxv, pp. 437-445.

Nichols (J.), London Pageants. *Gentleman's Magazine*, 1824, part i, p. 227 ; part ii, pp. 113-118, 411-414, 514-518 ; 1825, part i, pp. 30-33, 131-135, 221-223, 321-324, 418-422, 593-595. [These valuable communications give a bibliographical account of these curious civic customs, and they have been reprinted, with additions and notes, in *Gentleman's Magazine Library (Manners and Customs)*, pp. 103-153. The earliest record of a pageant is that noticed in the *French Chronicle of London*, p. 250, as occurring in 1312.]

Norton (George), An Exposition of the Privileges of the City of London in regard to the claims of non-freemen to deal by wholesale within its jurisdiction. London, 1821. 8vo, pp. 72.

Pulling (Alexander), The Laws, Customs, Usages, and Regulations of the City and Port of London ; with notes of all the charters, ordinances, statutes, and cases. Second edition. To which is added a summary of the Commissioners' Report on the Corporation of London and the Municipal Government of the Metropolis, 1854, showing in what particulars the Laws and Customs of the City are proposed to be altered. London, no date [1854]. 8vo, pp. lxix, 580 ; appendix, 38.

Contents : Introduction. Chapter i, The Municipal Constitution of the City of London ; ii, The Lord Mayor ; iii, The Aldermen ; iv, The Common Council ; v, The Citizens of London ; vi, The Companies ; vii, The Livery; viii, The Property and Revenues of the Corporation of London, and the mode in which they are managed and disposed of ; ix, The Local Rates and Taxes ; x, The Ministerial Officers of the Corporation ; xi, The Sheriffs ; xii, The Police ; xiii, The Courts of Law belonging to the City of London ; xiv, The Gaols and Houses of Correction ; xv, The Maintenance and Relief of the Poor and Sick of London ; xvi, The Laws relating to Tithes, Churches, Cemeteries, etc., in London ; xvii, Laws relating to Buildings in London ; xviii, Regulations of the Streets, Sewers, Lamps, and Aqueducts ; xix, The River Thames and Port of London ; xx, Pilots, Watermen, and Lightermen ; xxi, The Quays, Wharfs, and Docks, and Regulations of the Custom House ; xxii, The Civic Regulations as to Trade in London ; xxiii, The Public Markets in London ; xxiv, The Royal Exchange and Regulations as to Brokers, etc. ; xxv, The Bankers' Regulations and the Money Market ; xxvi, The Stock and Share

Market ; xxvii, The Shipping and Insurance Regulations in London ; xxviii, Commercial Sales ; xxix, The Corn Exchange ; xxx, The Coal Trade ; xxxi, The Retail Trade in London, and the Customs as to Apprentices and Femes covert ; xxxii, The Laws relating to Victuallers and Tavern Keepers in London ; xxxiii, Porters, Carriers, and Coachmen in London.

Riley (Henry Thomas), Mediæval Chronicles of the City of London. Chronicles of the Mayors and Sheriffs of London, and the Events which happened in their days, from the year A.D. 1188 to A.D. 1274. Translated from the original Latin of the " Liber de Antiquis Legibus" (published by the Camden Society), in the possession of the Corporation of the City of London ; attributed to Arnold Fitz-Thedmar, Alderman of London in the reign of Henry III.—Chronicles of London, and of the Marvels therein, between the years 44 Henry III, A.D. 1260, and 17 Edward III, A.D. 1343. Translated from the original Anglo-Norman of the "Croniques de London," preserved in the Cottonian Collection (Cleopatra A. iv) in the British Museum. Translated, with copious Notes and Appendices. London, 1863. 4to, pp. xii, 319.

—————— Munimenta Gildhallæ Londoniensis : Liber Albus, Liber Custumarum, et Liber Horn. London, 1859-1862. 3 vols., 8vo.

Vol. i, containing Liber Albus, A.D. 1419,

pp. cxxxi, 741. Vol. ii, 2 parts, containing
Liber Custumarum, with extracts from the
Cottonian MS. Claudius, D.H. pp. cxlvii,
432 ; 433-897. Vol. iii, containing translation of the Anglo-Norman passages in Liber
Albus, Glossaries, Appendices, and Index,
pp. xiii, 529.

Riley (Henry Thomas), Liber Albus: the White
Book of the City of London, compiled A.D.
1419, by John Carpenter, common clerk, and
Richard Whitington, Mayor; translated from
the original Latin and Anglo-Norman. London, 1861. 4to, pp. x, 660.

Royal (The) Charter of Confirmation granted
by the King Charles II to the City of London, wherein are recited verbatim all the
Charters to the said city granted by his
Majesties Royal Predecessors, Kings and
Queens of England. Taken out of the Records and exactly translated into English by
S. G., Gent. Together with an Index or
Alphabetical Table, and a Table explaining
all the obsolete and difficult words in the said
charter. London [1663]. 12mo, pp. 11 leaves
and 247.

Schultes (Henry), An Inquiry into the Elective
Franchise of the Citizens of London and the
General Rights of the Livery. London, 1822.
8vo, pp. 56 and Index. [An important pamphlet on early municipal customs.]

S., M. [Moses Stringer], Opera Mineralia Explicata; or, the Mineral Kingdom within the dominions of Great Britain displayed: being a compleat History of the Antient Corporations of the City of London; of and for the Mines, the Mineral and the Battery Works; with the original Grants, Leases, Instruments, Writs of Privilege and Protection by Sea and Land from Arrest (except in the Mineral Courts); or being prest, or serving juries and parish officers; as also the Records of the said Mineral Courts from the Conquest down to this present year, 1713. London [1713]. 12mo, pp. xii, 308.

Ludlow :

Copies of the Charters and Grants to the town of Ludlow, with a mirror for the men of Ludlow; illustrating their Corporation rights, an account of charitable foundations, three ancient descriptions of Ludlow, copies of Magna Charta, Bill of Rights, Habeas Corpus and the Act of Settlement; and extracts from Mr. Sharp's Essay on the Ancient Right of Election. Ludlow, 1821. 8vo.

Lynn Regis :

Dashwood (Rev. G. H.), Extracts from the Chamberlain's Book of Accounts, 14 Hen. IV, in the possession of the Corporation of Lynn Regis. *Norfolk and Norwich Arch. Soc.*, ii, 183-192.

Turner (Dawson), Copies and Translations of Two Deeds in the possession of the Corporation of Lynn. *Norfolk and Norwich Arch. Soc.*, ii, 193-197.

Maidenhead :

Gorham (G. C.), An Account of the Chapel Chauntry and Gild of Maidenhead, with a few particulars of the Parishes of Cookham and Bray. London, 1838. 8vo.

Maidstone :

Gilbert (Walter B.), The Accounts of the Corpus Christi Fraternity, and Papers relating to the Antiquities of Maidstone ; together with a list of mayors and other corporate officers from the earliest times. Maidstone, 1865. 8vo.

James (W. R.), The Charters and other Documents relating to the King's town and parish of Maidstone, in the county of Kent ; with notes and annotations clearly showing the right of election of members of Parliament to be vested in the inhabited householders. London, 1825. 8vo, pp. xxi, 238.

Maldon :

Addresses and Correspondence of Col. J. Strutt, respecting the Charter of Maldon. [Plate of seals.] Privately printed. 1812. 8vo.

Manchester :

Mamecestre ; being chapters from the early recorded history of the barony ; the lordship or manor, the vill, borough, or town of Manchester. Edited by John Harland. (Chetham Society.) Manchester, 1861. 4to, 3 vols., pp. 626.

A Volume of Court Leet Records of the Manor of Manchester in the 16th century. Compiled and edited by John Harland. (Chetham Society.) Manchester, 1864. 4to, pp. xix, 208.

Continuation of the Court Leet Records of the Manor of Manchester, A.D. 1586-1602. Compiled and \edited by John Harland. Manchester, 1865. 4to, pp. viii, 128.

The Manchester Historical Recorder; being an analysis of the municipal, ecclesiastical, biographical, commercial, and statistical history of Manchester. Manchester, 1874. 12mo.

City of Manchester : Chronicle of the City Council from incorporation, October 1838, to September 1879. Manchester, 1880. 8vo.

Marlborough :

,ᶦ Carrington (F. A.), Ancient Seals of the Borough of Marlborough. *Wilts Arch. and Nat. Hist. Soc.*, iii, pp. 114-115.

Monmouth :

The Charters of the Town and Borough of Monmouth. Newport, 1826. 8vo.

New Lymington :

Records of the Corporation of the Borough of New Lymington, extracted from the monuments in the possession of the mayor and other authorities, by C. St. Barbe. London, 1848. 4to.

Newcastle-on-Tyne :

The Report of the Select Committee of Burgesses of Newcastle-upon-Tyne, relative to the intended Act of Parliament for the Improvement of the Town Moor, Castle leazes, and Nun's Moor. Newcastle-upon-Tyne, 1811. 8vo.

Brown (J.), A Short Account of the Customs and Franchises of the Freemen of Newcastle-upon-Tyne, with an appendix containing the charter of Elizabeth, the charter of James, the Town Moor Act. Newcastle, 1823.

Extracts from the Municipal Accounts of Newcastle-upon-Tyne, extending from 1561 to the Revolution of 1688. Newcastle, 1849. 8vo.

Extracts from the Municipal Accounts of Newcastle-upon-Tyne. Reprints of Rare Tracts and Imprints of Antient Manuscripts, etc., chiefly illustrative of the history of the northern counties, and printed at the press of M. A. Richardson, Newcastle [n. d.], pp. 1-122.

Bell (John), Collections for a History of the Municipal Government of the Borough, Town and County of Newcastle-upon-Tyne, and its Conservancy of the River. [Newcastle-upon-Tyne, 1733-1855.] Fol. [This volume is in the British Museum, and consists of docu-

ments, MSS., and extracts from newspapers,
etc., extending from 1733 to 1855.]

Collier (John), An Essay on Charters ; in which
are particularly considered those of Newcastle. Newcastle, 1777. 8vo.

Newport :

Morgan (Octavius), The Early Charters of the
Borough of Newport in Wentloog. *Archæologia,* xlviii, pp. 431-455.

Northampton :

An Account of the Surrender of the Old Charter
of Northampton, and the manner of their re-
ceiving their New Charter. London, 1686.
Sheet folio.

Hartshorne (Rev. C. H.), Historical Memorials
of Northampton, taken chiefly from unprinted
records. Northampton and London, 1848.
12mo, pp. 25.

Contents: The Charters—Extract from the
Chamberlain's Book of Minutes—Municipal
Archives—The Castle and Parliament—
Queen Eleanor's Cross — The Religious
Houses in Northampton—The Mint—The
Fire.

Norwich :

Extracts from original Manuscripts belonging
to the Norwich Corporation, and other documents. *Norfolk and Norwich Arch. Soc.,* i,
1-40.

Ewing (W. C.), Remarks on the Boundary of

the City and Hamlets of Norwich. *Norfolk and Norwich Arch. Soc.*, ii, 1-16.

Harrod (Henry), Extracts from the Coroners' Rolls and other documents in the Record Room of the Corporation of Norwich. *Norfolk and Norwich Arch. Soc.*, ii, 253-279.

Nottingham :

Records of the Borough of Nottingham, being a series of extracts from the archives of the Corporation of Nottingham, published under the authority of the Corporation of Nottingham. London and Nottingham, 1882-1883. Vol. i, 1155-1399, pp. xvi, 487 ; vol. ii, 1399-1485, pp. xx, 509.

Heathcote (C.), An English Translation of the Charter of Henry VI to the Burgesses of the Town and County of Nottingham, confirmed to them by letters patent of King William and Queen Mary, to which is prefixed an Introductory Address to the burgesses of the said town. Nottingham, 1807. Folio.

Oxford :

Turner (William H.), Selections from the Records of the City of Oxford, with extracts from other documents illustrating the municipal history — Henry VIII to Elizabeth, 1509-1583. Oxford and London, 1880. 8vo, pp. xl, 478.

Contents: Preface ; i, Entries and Documents concerning the Controversies between

the City and the University as to Jurisdiction ; ii, Entries and Documents connected
with the routine business of the City ; iii,
List of Officers of the City ; iv, Regulations
respecting the Trades and Crafts of the Town;
v, The Presentation to the City Churches ;
vi, Enrolments of Deeds in the "Liber Albus",
and other documents chiefly referring to lands
and tenements in or near Oxford.

Peebles :

Scottish Burgh Records Society. Charters and
Documents relating to the Burgh of Peebles,
with extracts from the Records of the Burgh,
A.D. 1165-1710. Edinburgh, 1872. 4to, pp.
lxxv, 456.

Pevensey :

Larking (Rev. L. B.), Custumal of Pevensey, as
delivered to the Lord Warden at Dover Castle
in 1356. *Suss. Arch. Coll.*, iv, 209-218.

Plymouth :

Plimouth Memoirs, containing a chronologicall
account of that corporation, a catalogue of
all the mayors, togather with ye memorable
occurrences in their respective yeares, the
oaths taken by severall officers in said corporation, particularly of the freemen, both befor
and upon ye Regulation, 1684, the charter
then granted by K. Charles the Second, etc.
Collected by James Yonge, 1684. Edited by
R. N. Worth. Plymouth, 1876. 8vo, pp. 58.

Jewett (Llewellyn), The Maces, Loving Cups, and Corporation Insignia of Plymouth. *Reliquary*, 1877-8, vol. xviii, 97-8.

Pontefract :

Holmes (Richard), The Booke of Entries of the Pontefract Corporation, 1653-1726. Pontefract, 1882. 8vo, pp. 434.

Preston :

Addison (John), Extracts from Ancient Documents in the Archives of the Corporation of Preston. 1842.

Taylor (John), A Brief Description of the Burrough and Town of Preston, and its Government and Guild. Originally composed between 1682 and 1686. Preston, 1818. 8vo.

The Charters granted by different Sovereigns to the Burgesses of Preston. Printed from attested copies, etc. Preston, 1821. 8vo, 2 pts.

Prestwich :

Maitland Club. Records of the Burgh of Prestwich in the Sheriffdom of Ayr. MCCCCLXX-MDCCLXXXII; with an appendix and illustrative notes. Glasgow, 1834. 4to, pp. xxvii, 147. [The Prefatory Notice is signed J. F.]

Rochester :

Authentic Copy of the Charter and Bye-laws of the City of Rochester. 1749. Fol.

St. Albans :

Black (W. H.), On the Town Records of St.

Albans. *Journ. Arch. Assoc.*, xxvi, 143-149.

Farrington (Serjt. E.), Charters of St. Albans. 1813. 8vo.

Salisbury :

[Easton (J.)], A Correct List of the Mayors of New Sarum, or Salisbury, with an introductory account relative to the foundation of the city. Salisbury, 1826. 8vo.

Southampton :

Charter to Southampton, 1641. London, 1810. 12mo.

Vaux (W. S. W.), Some Notices of Records preserved amongst the Corporation Archives at Southampton. *Arch. Journ.*, iii, 229-233.

Stratford-upon-Avon :

Halliwell (James O.), A descriptive Calendar of the Ancient Manuscripts and Records in the possession of the Corporation of Stratford-upon-Avon ; including notices of Shakespeare and his family, and of several persons connected with the poet. London (privately printed), 1863. Folio, pp. viii, 467.

—— A brief hand list of the Records belonging to the Borough of Stratford-on-Avon, showing their general character, with notes of a few of the Shakespearian documents in the same collection. Privately printed, 1862. 4to, pp. 32.

—— Extracts from the Accounts of the

Chamberlains of the Borough of Stratford-upon-Avon, from the year 1585 to 1608. Selected and edited from the original manuscripts. Privately printed, 1866. 8vo, pp. 46.

Halliwell (James O.), Extracts from the Accounts of the Chamberlains of the Borough of Stratford-upon-Avon, from 1609 to 1619. London, 1867, 4to.

—— Stratford-upon-Avon in the Times of the Shakespeares, illustrated by extracts from the Council Books of the Corporation, selected especially with reference to the history of the poet's father. Illustrated with facsimiles of the entries respecting John Shakespeare. Privately printed, 1864. Folio, pp. 127.

Swansea :

Francis (George Grant), Charters granted to Swansea, the chief Borough of the Seignory of Gower in the Marches of Wales and County of Glamorgan. Translated, illustrated, and edited. London, 1867. 4to.

—— Notes on a Gold Chain of Office presented to the Corporation of Swansea in 1875, with a list of the gentlemen who have filled the office of Mayor from 1835 to 1875. Swansea, 1876. 8vo.

Tenby :

Property and Revenues of the Corporation of the Borough of Tenby, in the years 1835 and 1839. Parliamentary paper, 1840 (611), xli, 545.

Totnes :

Amery (John S.), The Accounts of the Receiver of the Corporation of Totnes in the year 1554-5. *Transactions of Devonshire Association*, vol. xii, pp. 322-331.

Dymond (R.), Ancient Documents relating to the Civil History of Totnes. *Transactions of Devonshire Association*, vol. xii, pp. 192-203.

Warwick :

The Governing Charter of the Borough of Warwick, with a Letter to the Burgesses, by Joseph Parkes. 1827. 8vo.

Winchelsea :

Bray (William), A Letter to the Mayor and Jurats of the Town of Winchelsea respecting the choice of Officers in that Corporation, A.D. 1609. *Archæologia*, vol. xviii, 291-293.

Winchester :

Bailey (Charles), Transcripts from the Municipal Archives of Winchester, and other documents; elucidating the government, manners, and customs of the same city, from the thirteenth century to the present period. Winchester, 1856. 8vo.

Smirke (E), Ancient Consuetudinary of the City of Winchester. *Arch. Journ.*, vol. ix, pp. 69-89.

Wycombe (Chipping) :

Charters and Grants relating to Chipping Wycombe. 1817. 4to.

Yarmouth :

Repertory of Deeds and Documents relating to the Borough of Great Yarmouth. Great Yarmouth, 1855. 4to. [King John's Charter is photographed.]

York :

A List or Catalogue of all the Mayors and Bailiffs, Lord Mayors and Sheriffs of the City of York to the year 1664. York, 1715. 8vo.

Torr (James), Antiquities of York City, and the City Government thereof, with a list of the mayors, sheriffs, etc., from Edward I to 1719. York, 1719. 8vo.

Davies (Robert), Extracts from the Municipal Records of the City of York during the reigns of Edward IV, Edward V, and Richard III, with notes illustrative and explanatory, and an appendix containing some account of the celebration of the Corpus Christi festival at York in the fourteenth, fifteenth, and sixteenth centuries. London, 1843. 8vo, pp. vii, 304.

L

V.—GILDS.

THE value of Gild Records cannot be over-rated. Not only do they throw light upon a most important portion of social history during the middle ages, but to a very considerable extent they form the materials for the mediæval history of commerce We have in these old documents, too, besides their historical value, remnants of an archaic mode of life which appears to me to stretch far back into times which precede the age of historians. If I am right in this view, no time should be lost in getting together all that remains of gild history and records in the country, for it is curious to note that gilds exist not only in municipal towns, where they have thriven most of all, but in towns which have never had, so far as can be ascertained, any municipal constitution.

As to the origin of gilds much has been written, and Mr. Coote, in his *Romans of*

Britain, boldly claims them as the direct
descendants of the Roman "collegia". But
I think their true origin must be found in
a much earlier institution than the late-
developed Roman collegium, and this, I
cannot help thinking, is the archaic family
—joint in food, worship, and estate—which
meets us on the threshold of all early
Indo-European history. The Anglo-Saxon
family has not yet met with its historian,
except in one of the interesting and valuable
Essays in Anglo-Saxon Law (Boston.
1876), where Mr. Ernest Young writes on
"The Anglo-Saxon family law". But even
in the family as it is to be seen dimly
in the chronicle narratives and in the legal
codes of the Anglo-Saxons, there are strong
traces of its fundamental adherence to the
archaic type to be found elsewhere, and it
is to this that I would look for the origin
of the gild. The gild found in the archaic
family, at all events, its organisation and
its vitality ; and when kinship gave way
before commerce, the latter took advantage
of this natural organisation to promote and

foster its far-reaching ends. We meet with the very process going on in modern Russia, and it will be well for one moment to turn to this important phase of the question as guide.

In Russia, where the family ties in their primitive characteristics are still very strong, commerce has been grappled with in a singularly instructive way. " When one of the sons left home to work elsewhere, he was expected to bring or send home all his earnings except what he required for food, lodgings, and other necessary expenses. . . . During his absence his wife and children remained in the house as before."[1] This, no doubt, is the beginning of the break-up of the family. But let us see a more primitive state of things. " Very often the peasants find industrial occupation without leaving home. . . . Occasionally we find not only a whole village, but even a whole district, occupied almost exclusively with some one kind of manual industry. . . . These domestic industries

[1] Wallace's *Russia*, i, 135.

have long existed. . . . The head of the household bought the raw material, and sold with a reasonable profit the manufactured articles at the local fairs."[1] Nothing could be more instructive in the right understanding of primitive economic history than this. The family in this latter case is collective in commercial as in agricultural pursuits. In the former case the communal system is kept up by the payment of earnings to the family chest. But even when this occurs, the sons form themselves, in their character of workmen, into collective units under the name of artéls. "The artél in its various forms is a curious institution", says Mr. Wallace.[2] "They were simply temporary itinerant associations of workmen, who during the summer lived together, fed together, worked together, and on the termination of each bit of work, divided amongst themselves the profits."

Now in these phases of primitive economic history, I think we have the

---

[1] Wallace's *Russia*, 155-156.   [2] *Ibid.*, 132.

germ of the later gild history—the germ only, not the full growth. In course of time it became linked to the great centres of all commercial prosperity, namely, the municipal boroughs ; and when it reached this point, it is not difficult to trace the gradual approach of the gild to the burghal community, the gradual amalgamation of both into the municipal corporation of modern times, or according to the views of Mr. Coote, in reference to London,[1] the ultimate overturning of the old burghal constitution in favour of the gild constitution. There is much dispute as to the exact period when the merchant gild merged into the corporation. Mr. Thompson (*English Municipal History*, Introd., p. x), suggests that the reign of Elizabeth marked the era, but my own opinion would suggest a much earlier date —a point, however, that can only be properly settled by a study of the important literature which this interesting subject has produced. One of the most remark-

---

[1] *Secular Gilds of London*, p. 22.

able pieces of evidence which I have come across is from the records of the Gild of Totnes, dated 1260. Admissions to the gild seem to have been obtained by purchase, gift, or *relationship*, and the description of some of the chief formalities of the gild, given in the *Third Report of the Historical MSS. Commission* (p. 342), is very curious. From the great care taken in defining the sittings of the members of the gild, it seems not improbable that a certain seat or place was assigned to each trader in the open market of the town, a corresponding seat being assigned in the church as well. The whole record reminds one of a trading community two or three stages of development beyond the Russian artél. The obligations to the community are kept up by the gild payments and the occupation of gild seats, whereas the new departure towards individual rights is marked by the influences of purchase and gift, alongside of the older influences of relationship, while the allotment of church seats brings the whole institution within the compass of the old formula already quoted—joint in food, worship, and estate.

But it is not possible to dwell upon so complicated and fascinating a subject as the origin of gilds within the limits now available. It is enough, perhaps, to have pointed out that the last word has not yet been written, and that scholarly and important as Dr. Brentano's famous treatise on the subject is, modern research will enable much more definite conclusions to be drawn than was possible fifteen years ago. There is a fairly extensive literature upon this section of our subject, and there are vast treasures still remaining in MSS.

Aberdeen : An Inquiry into the Rights of the Guildry of Aberdeen. By Mr. Thomas Bannerman, the Dean of Guild. March 1834. Aberdeen : printed by John Davidson & Co., MDCCCXXXIV. 8vo, pp. xvi, 130.

—— Notes on Mr. Bannerman's *Inquiry into the Rights of the Guildry of Aberdeen.* By A. Burgess. August 1834. Aberdeen : printed at the *Herald* Office, by G. Cornwall, 1834. 8vo, pp. 34.

Aberdeen: Report on the Affairs of the Guildry of Aberdeen, ordered by a head court of the Brethren, 5th October 1835. By a Committee of Assessors. Aberdeen: printed at the *Herald* Office, by G. Cornwall. 1836. 8vo, pp. 168.

—— Letter to the Burgesses of Guild of the City of Aberdeen, regarding the state of their affairs ; with suggestions as to the course to be pursued by them. By Leslie Clark, Dean of Guild. Aberdeen : printed at the *Herald* Office, by John Finlayson. 1839. 8vo, pp. 28.

—— Report of the Committee of the Dean of Guild's Assessors, appointed to inquire into the state of the funds appertaining to the Guild Brethren, to the Dean of Guild and Assessors. March 1834. Aberdeen : printed by D. Chalmers & Co., 25, Adelphi Court, Union Street. 1834. 8vo, pp. 12.

Abram (W. A.), Memorials of the Preston Guilds, illustrating the manner in which the Guild Merchant has been held in the Borough from the Earliest on Record until the Last Guild in 1862. Preston, 1882. Royal 4to.

Amery (P. F. S.), The Gild Merchant of Totnes. *Trans. of Devonshire Association*, vol. xii, pp. 179-191.

Arber (Edward), Transcript of the Registers of the Company of Stationers of London, 1554-1640. London, 1875-7. 4to, 4 vols.

Archæologia : a particular note of suche charytable good uses as are performed by divers of the Companies of London out of suche rentes as they purchased of King Edward VIth. *Archæologia*, vol. xxxi, pp. 386.

Arundell (Thomas), Historical Reminiscences of the City of London and its Livery Companies.   London, 1869.   8vo, pp. xii, 444.

Contents : The Livery Companies—Their Origin and Objects—Their Antiquity—Their Aldermen—Their Mayor—Their Sheriffs—Their Name Livery—Their Religious Observances—Their Apprenticeship—Feasts in Olden Time—Crowning with Garlands—Minstrels—The Loving Cup and Players—Their Maidens—Their Holidays—Their Mayings—Royal Processions—Lord Mayor's Day—Water Pageants — Out-door Games—Their Fondness for Dirt in the Olden Times—The Twelve City Ceremonials—The Relation of the Companies to Trade—Their Modern Banquets — Their Armorial Bearings — Their Training to Arms—Their Warriors—List of Mayors from 1189 to 1869—Lord Mayors M.P. for the City—Lord Mayors M.P. for the Provinces—List of Charters from William the Conqueror to George III—Index.

Black (W. H.), History and Antiquities of the Worshipful Companies of Leathersellers of the City of London.   London, 1871.

Bower (S.), The Arms of the Principal Companies of the City of London.   1698.

Brentano (Lujo), On the History and Develop-

ment of Gilds, and the Origin of Trade
Unions. London, 1870. 8vo, pp. xvi, 135.

Contents : 1, The Origin of Gilds ; 2, Re-
ligious (or Social) Gilds ; 3, Town Gilds or
Gild Merchants ; 4, Craft-Gilds ; 5, Trade
Unions. [A reprint of the Introduction to
Toulmin Smith's *The Gilds*, published by
the Early English Text Society.]

Bristol : Guild of Calendaries at Bristol. *Gentleman's Magazine*, 1789, part ii, p. 993.

Cheesewright (R. J.), A Short Account of the
Worshipful Company of Cutlers. London,
1882.

[Clode (Charles Mathew)], Memorials of the
Guild of Merchant Taylors of the Fraternity
of St. John the Baptist in the City of London,
and of its associated Charities and Institutions. Compiled and selected by the Master of
the Company for the year 1873-4 (being the
574th Master in succession). London, 1875.
8vo, pp. xxxi, 746.

Compton (C. H.), The Horners of the City of
London. *Journ. Arch. Assoc.*, xxxv, pp. 372-9.

Cooper (W. D.), Guild and Chantries in Horsham. *Suss. Arch. Coll.*, xxii, 148-59.

Coote (Henry Charles), Ordinances of some
Secular Guilds of London, from 1354 to 1496;
to which are added ordinances of St. Marga-
ret Lothbury, 1456, and orders by Richard,
Bishop of London, for ecclesiastical officers,

1597, by John Robert Daniel-Tyssen. London, 1871. 8vo, pp. 93.

Coote (Henry Charles), London Notes : The English Gilds of Knights and their Socn. *London and Middlesex Arch. Soc.*, vol. v.

Cotton (William), An Elizabethan Guild of the City of Exeter. London, 1873. 4to, pp. 179.

Daw (Joseph), Sketch of the Early History of the Worshipful Company of Butchers. London, 1869.

Dobson (William) and John Harland, F.S.A., A History of Preston Guild ; the Ordinances of various Guilds Merchant, the Custumal of Preston, the Charters to the Borough, the Incorporated Companies, List of Mayors from 1327, etc., etc. Preston [no date]. 12mo, pp. 115.

The items covered by the etc., etc., of the title-page are the Corporation Regalia, the Preston Guild. and the Incorporated Trades, a Ballad of the Guild of 1802.

Dobson (W.), An Account of the Celebration of Preston Guild in 1862. Preston, 1862. 12mo.

[Firth (James F.)], Coopers' Company, London : Historical Memoranda, Charters, Documents, and Extracts from the Records of the Corporation and the Books of the Company, 1396-1848. London, 1848. 8vo. pp. 136.

Fitch (W. S.), Notices of the Corpus Christi

Guild, Ipswich. *Suffolk Arch. Inst.,* ii, 151-163.

Fox (Francis F.), Some account of the Ancient Fraternity of Merchant Taylors of Bristol, with transcripts of ordinances and other documents. Bristol, 1880. [Fifty copies privately printed.] 4to, pp. 147.

Franks (Robert H.), A Letter to Lord Althorp on the Justice and Necessity of Reforming the Livery Companies of London. 1833.

Gillespy (Thomas), Some Account of the Worshipful Company of Salters. London, 1827.

Gross (Dr. Charles), Gilda Mercatoria ; ein Beitrag zur Geschichte der englishchen städteverfassung. Göttingen, 1883. 8vo, pp. vi, 109.

Heath (John Benjamin), Some Account of the Worshipful Company of Grocers of the City of London. London, 1829. (Not published.) 8vo, pp. viii, 358.

—— The same, second edition. London, 1854. [Privately printed.] 4to, pp. xvi, 580. [Contains an Appendix of important original documents not given in the first edition.]

—— The same, third edition. London, 1869. [Privately printed.] 8vo, pp. xvi, 601.

Herbert (William), The History of the Twelve Great Livery Companies of London ; principally compiled from their grants and records; with an historical essay, and accounts of each company, its origin, constitution, government, dress, customs, halls, and trust estates and charities, including notices and illustrations of Metropolitan Trade and Commerce, as originally concentrated in those societies ; and of the language, manners, and expenses of ancient times ; with attested copies and translations of the Companies' Charters. London : vol. i, 1837 ; vol. ii, 1836. 2 vols., 8vo, pp. xi, 498 ; viii, 683.

Contents : Historical Essay — Separate Histories of the Companies—Mercers, Grocers, Drapers, Fishmongers, Goldsmiths, Skinners, Merchant Taylors, Haberdashers, Salters, Ironmongers, Vintners, Clothworkers.

Humphries (Henry). History of the Origin and Progress of the Watermen's Company, 1514-1859. London, 2 vols., 1878-1883.

Jervise (Andrew), Inscriptions from the Shields, or Panels, of the Incorporated Trades in the Trinity Hall, Aberdeen, including notices of the antique carved oak chairs, etc. 1863. 8vo.

Jupp (Edward Basil), An Historical Account of the Worshipful Company of Carpenters of the City of London, compiled chiefly from records in their possession. London, 1848. 8vo, pp. xix, 338. ["The first to attempt anything like a detailed history of any particular Company."—*Pref.*]

Kingdon (J. A.), Facsimiles of Early Ordinances, Minute and Account Books, etc., of the

Grocers' Company, 1345-1423; supplemented by extracts from the Corporation Records. London, 1883. [Privately printed.]

Kite (Edward), The Guild of Merchants or Trading Companies formerly existing in Devizes. *Wilts Arch. and Nat. Hist. Soc.*, iv, 160-174.

Lambert (G.), The Barbers' Company: a paper read before the British Archæological Association at Barber Surgeon's Hall, Monkwell Street, on Saturday, October 5th, 1881. London, 1881. 8vo, pp. 67.

Latchford (Benjamin), The Loriner: Opinions and Observations on Bridle Bits, etc. London, 1871. [The appendix contains ordinances and other documents relating to the Company of Loriners.]

Laws and Constitutions of the Masters, Wardens, and Commonalty of Watermen of the River Thames. By the Court of Mayor and Aldermen of the City of London. London, 1828. 8vo, pp. xii, 85.

Little (William Charles), An Historical Account of the Hammermen of Edinburgh, from their Records. *Arch. Scot.*, vol. i, pp. 170-183.

Loggon (J.), The History of the Brotherhood or Guild of the Holy Ghost in the Chapel of the Holy Ghost, near Basingstoke, in Hampshire. Reading, 1742. 8vo.

London : City of London Livery Companies

Commission. Report and Appendix. London, 1884. Fol. [blue book]. Vol. i, containing (1) the Reports and Memoranda of the Commissioners ; and (2) the Oral Inquiry. Vol. ii.

Ludlow (J. M.), Gilds and Friendly Societies. *Contemporary Review*, 1873. vol. xxi, pp. 553-72, 737-62.

Mackie (A. K.), Historical Notes regarding the Merchant Company of Edinburgh and the Widows' Scheme and Hospitals. Edinburgh, 1862. 4to, pp. 128; appendix, xlviii. [Privately printed by Charles Lawson, Master of the Company, upon his retirement.]

Mitchell (Robert), Sketches of a Glasgow Incorporation [Maltmen and Mealmen]. *Glasgow Arch. Soc.*, i, 420-437.

Morley (Timothy), Some Account of the Company of Armourers and Braziers. London, 1878.

Needlemakers : The Worshipful Company of Needlemakers of the City of London, with a list of the Court of Assistants and Livery. London, 1874. 4to, pp. 90.

Nicholl (John), Some Account of the Worshipful Company of Ironmongers, compiled from their own Records and other authentic sources of information. London, 1851. Roy. 8vo, pp. vi, 610.

—— The same, second edition. London,

1866. [Privately printed.] 4to, pp. xii, 657. [The principal additions consist of pedigrees of members and benefactors.]

Nichols (John Gough), The Fishmongers' Pageant on Lord Mayor's Day, 1616. Chrysanaleia, the Golden Fishing, devised by Anthony Munday, citizen and draper, represented in twelve plates by Henry Shaw, F.S.A., from contemporary drawings in the possession of the Worshipful Company of Fishmongers, accompanied with various illustrative documents, and an historical introduction. Printed for the Worshipful Company of Fishmongers, 1844. Large folio, pp. 32 and 12 plates.

—— Coat Armour of the Fishmongers and Goldsmiths. London, 1859.

Norris (Edward S.), A Short History of the Curriers' Company. 1874.

Oldisworth (Austin), The Armorial Bearings of the twelve chief Companies of the City of London. 1701.

Overall (William Henry), F.S.A. [Librarian to the Corporation of the City of London], and Samuel Elliott Atkins [formerly Clerk of the Company], Some account of the Worshipful Company of Clockmakers of the City of London, compiled principally from their own records and those of the Blacksmiths' Company. London, 1881. 8vo. [Privately printed.] Index, pp. xvii; Introduction, pp. v, 346.

M

Contents : Introduction, The Company :—
Charter and Bye-laws — Arms — Seals —
Badges—Colours—Court of Assistants—The
Livery—Freemen—Apprentices— Biographi-
cal Notices of Members—Meeting Places—
Feasts—Archives—Plate — Charities — Gifts
to the Company—The Trade :—Regulations
of Workmen—Searches—Patents and Inven-
tions — Importation and Exportation of
Watches and Clocks—False Working—Hall
Marking.

Pennecuik (A.), Blue Blanket ; or, Craftsmen's
Banner: An Historical Sketch of the Municipal
Constitution of the City of Edinburgh, includ-
ing the Set of the Burgh as established in
1583 and amended in 1730 ; with the Acts of
Parliament and Council relating thereto, and
Lists of the Aldermen and Lord Provosts,
Magistrates, Deacon-Conveners, the Council,
Representatives in Parliament, Masters of
the Merchant Company, Moderators of the
High Constables, etc., from the earliest time
to the year 1826. To which is added, An
Historical Account of the Blue Blanket, or
the Craftsmen's Banner, containing the
Fundamental Principles of the Good Town,
with the Power and Prerogatives of the Crafts
of Edinburgh, etc. Edinburgh, 1826. Sm. 8vo.

—— The History of the Blue Blanket or
Craftsmen's Banner, containing the fundamental principles of the good town of Edinburgh, with the powers and prerogatives of

the Crafts thereof. Edinburgh, 1832. 8vo, pp. vii, 141.

Pettigrew (T. J.), History of the Barber-Surgeons of London. *Journ. Arch. Assoc.*, viii, 95-130.

Trade Guilds of the City of London. *Fraser's Magazine*, April 1879, vol. xix (n. s.), 395-405.

Pidgeon (Henry), Ancient Guilds, Trading Companies, and the Origin of the Shrewsbury Show. *Reliquary*, 1862-3, vol. iii, pp. 61-73.

Preston, An Account of the Guild Merchant of Preston. Preston, 1762. 8vo, pp. 18. [Pp. 9-18 are occupied by a list of the nobility and gentry who appeared at the balls and assemblies at Preston Guild, September 1762.]

—— The Guild Merchant of Preston, with an extract of the Original Charter granted for holding the same ; an account of the processions and public entertainments ; an authentic list of the nobility and gentry who dined with the Mayor and his Lady ; also separate lists of the subscribers to the Ladies' and Trade Assemblies. Preston [1762]. 8vo, pp. 38.

—— The History of Preston in Lancashire, together with the Guild Merchant, and some account of the Duchy and County Palatine of Lancaster. London, 1822. 8vo.

—— Preston Guild. *Lonsdale Magazine*, vol. iii (1822), pp. 269-73, 344-54.

Ravenhill (William), A short Account of the Company of Grocers, from their original, together with their case and condition . . . . as also how their revenue is settled . . . . London : printed by Eliz. Holt for the Company of Grocers, 1589. 4to.

Reader (W.), The Origin and Description of Coventry Show Fair and Peeping Tom. Coventry, 1824. 12mo.

Register (The) of the Gild of Corpus Christi in the City of York ; with an appendix of illustrative documents containing some account of the Hospital of St. Thomas of Canterbury, without Micklegate bar, in the suburbs of the city. Surtees Society : Durham, London, and Edinburgh, 1872. 8vo, pp. xiv, 362.

Robins (E. C.), Some Account of the History and Antiquities of the Worshipful Company of Dyers. *London and Mid. Arch. Soc.*, vol. v, pp. 441-76.

Rogers (Rev. Henry), The Calendars of Al-Hallowen Brystowe : an attempt to elucidate some portions of the history of the Priory of Fraternitie of Calendars, whose library once stood over the north or Jesus aisle of All Saints' Church, Bristol. Bristol, 1846. Pp. xi, 279.

Rules and Byelaws for the regulation of the Watermen and Lightermen of the River Thames. By the Court of Mayor and Aldermen of the City of London. London, 1828. 8vo, pp. v, 48.

Scriveners : The Case of the Free Scriveners of London, set forth in a Report from a Committee of the Court of Assistants of the Company of Scriveners. London : to the Master, Wardens, and Assistants of the Company at their Court holden 23 day of June 1748. London, 1749. 4to, pp. 88.

Sharp (T.), The Pageant of the Company of Sheremen and Taylors in Coventry, as performed by them on the Festival of Corpus Christi; together with other pageants exhibited on occasion of several royal visits to that city. Coventry, 1817. 4to.

—— A Dissertation on the Pageants or Dramatic Mysteries anciently performed at Coventry by the Trading Companies of that city, etc. Coventry, 1825. 4to.

Skaife (R. H.), The Register of the Guild of Corpus Christi in the City of York ; with an appendix of illustrative documents containing some account of the hospital of St. Thomas of Canterbury, etc. Durham (Surtees Society), 1872. 8vo.

Smirke (Edward), Ancient Ordinances of the Gild Merchants of the Town of Southampton. *Arch. Journ.*, xvi, 283-96, 343-52.

Smith (Toulmin), English Gilds : the Original Ordinances of more than one hundred Early English Gilds ; together with ye olde usages of ye citie of Wynchestre ; the ordinances of Worcester; the office of the Mayor of Bristol; and the costomary of the Manor of Tetten-hall-Regis ; from original MSS. of the four-teenth and fifteenth centuries. Edited with notes by the late Toulmin Smith ; with an in-troduction and glossary, etc., by his daughter, Lucy Toulmin Smith, and a preliminary essay in five parts on the history and development of Gilds, by Lujo Brentano. London (Early English Text Society), 1870. 8vo, pp. cxcix, 483.

Symonds (Rev. G. E.), Thaxted and its Cutlers' Guild. *Reliquary*, vol. v, pp. 65-72.

Turner (Rev. Edward), The Merchant Guild of Chichester. *Suss. Arch. Coll.*, xv, 165-77.

—— The Ancient Merchant Guild of Lewes, and the subsequent municipal regulations of the town. *Suss. Arch. Coll.*, xxi, 90-107.

Wadmore (James Foster), Some Account of the History and Antiquity of the Worshipful Company of Skinners. London, 1876. 8vo. [This book is not at the British Museum.]

Walford (Cornelius), Gilds : their Origin, Con-stitution, Objects, and Later History. [Re-printed from vol. v of Insurance Cyclopedia. Printed for private circulation, 1879.] 8vo, pp. 57.

Walford (W. S.), Observations on a Grant of an Advowson of a Chantry to a Guild in 34 Hen. VI. *Arch.*, xxxviii (i), 135-48.

Walker (J.) and M. A. Richardson, The Armorial Bearings of the Incorporated Companies of Newcastle-upon-Tyne. 1824.

Wallis (Richard), London's Armoury accurately delineated in a display of all the Arms, Crests, Supporters, and Mottoes of every distinct Company in the honourable City of London. 1677.

Wilcockson (L.), Authentic Records of the Guild Merchant of Preston in the county palatine of Lancaster in the year 1822, with an introduction containing an historical dissertation on the origin of Guilds and a relation of all the different celebrations of the Guild Mercatoria of Preston of which any records remain. Preston, 1822. 8vo, pp. iv, 128.

Wilda (Wilhelm Eduard), Das Gildenwesen im Mittelalter. Berlin [1831]. 8vo, pp. xii, 386.

Williams (William Meade), Annals of the Worshipful Company of Founders of the City of London. [Privately printed, n. d.] 8vo, pp. xi, 291.

Wilson (J.), Cordwainers and Corvesors of Oxford. *Arch. Journ.*, vi, 146-59, 266-79.

Yeats (John), Guilds and their Functions. *Journ. of Society of Arts*, vol. xxi, pp. 178-86.

VI.—THE MANOR.

So far as historical records are concerned this section of our subject forms perhaps the richest. There are no documents so valuable to the historian as the old records of manorial courts, because they show, in an unexampled fashion, the earliest evidence of social and agricultural history which we possess. But, alas! very little has been done to get this material published and available for use. It has been urged over and over again by students of unquestioned authority, that the manor court rolls ought to be published. Mr. Kemble, writing in 1849, said, "It is deeply to be lamented that the *very early* customs found in the copies of court rolls in England have not been collected and published"; and one of the Commissioners on Historical Manuscripts, referring to some manor rolls he was then describing, speaks in the same strain (see vol. ii, p. 69).

Mr. Edward Peacock, again, has made a more direct appeal—alas! in vain—in the pages of the *Athenæum* for August 1879, and the following passages of his letter may be quoted :—

"The writer of the review of Mr. Turner's calendar of the charters in the Bodleian, which appears in the *Athenæum* of July 19th, draws attention to the importance of manor court rolls, and points out that they are often in the custody of those who do not understand their value, and who sometimes treat them 'as mere rubbish'. This is certainly no exaggeration. I have known instances in which such records have been wantonly destroyed, and have in my own possession at this moment several years of the court roll of a Lincolnshire manor, which I myself saved from the flames. There is no doubt whatever that important records of this class are perishing almost daily. Lords of manors and their stewards are, perhaps, not so much to blame for this as historical students are inclined to think. The importance of the kind of evidence these documents furnish is utterly unappreciated by the ordinary country squire and his solicitor. Enclosures, the alteration of the law with regard to copyhold tenures, and several other causes, have combined to render these old documents of little service for purely business purposes, and business purposes are the only ones for which it is conceived such things can be required. It would be out of place here if I were to enter in detail into the subject, but it should really be impressed on all persons who have the care of manor records that they are of value for almost every purpose for which ancient evidence is important. The true history of our land tenure can never be made out without an exhaustive examination of the rolls of many times and from various widely-separated parts of England. As genealogical evidence it is not easy to exaggerate their importance, as they often give legal proof of marriages and deaths centuries before parish registers begin. Wills, charters, and inventories are often enrolled upon them. They moreover furnish what are probably the best attainable materials for the history of surnames, and facts, which are simply invaluable as to the old nomenclature of streams, fields, enclosures, hills, and trees.

"If inquiries were instituted, and a list made of, as far as possible, all existing manor rolls, a great step would have been taken. If no other good came of it, their present custodians would have been informed, by an authority which they would respect, that their documents were not rubbish, but things highly curious and worthy of the most careful preservation."

The manor and the township are children of the same archaic parent—the village community. The former has taken all the essential parts of the older organisation, and has left the latter almost devoid of vitality, except such new vitality as the needs of the central government have called into being, by from time to time imposing new duties and calling upon it to assist in the increasing needs of the government of the

State. But while the central government has thus dealt with the township, it has left the manor entirely to itself. It has thus grown under the ever-increasing development of individual rights to become the appendage of chiefs and lords. Its principal characteristic has always been the possession of agricultural and land-owning rights and duties, and in the constitution of the so-called feudal manors, we can trace quite easily most of the features of the primitive village community, which in very early times consisted of a band of relations, real or assumed, who lived together, joint in food, worship, and estate, and who thus held property and rights in common, each villager being the equal fellow of his co-villagers. How these old rights have developed into lord's rights on the one hand, and tenants' rights on the other, is a long story, but it can be read in the books which are enumerated in this section. The subject is one of increasing interest to the historian and to the economist ; and when it touches upon so wide a question as

land owning, it will be seen how very great
indeed is the political interest also. We
have in our midst social reformers, who
would have us adopt the theoretical organisation advocated by the communists and
socialists, as they are termed ; and yet it is
not generally known that to adopt these
political principles would be to travel back
some thousand years of history. Our
earliest ancestors were socialists and communists by descent from early stages of
society ; but before they became Englishmen, and thought of empire and conquest
and civilisation, they threw off these social
surroundings, and stepped into the arena as
individuals in thought and action. By this
individualism we gained and triumphed in
the past, and it is a thought now worth
bearing in mind, whether to depart from it
would not lead us back to a condition of
things similar to that which kept those great
hordes of valiant men prone and helpless at
the feet of Rome for so many years.

It was once a well-supported assumption
that manors were introduced by the Nor-

mans, but later historical research opposes
this theory.   And yet, after all, it is only
a partial opposition.   Manors, as recognised
by lawyers, no doubt cannot be traced prior
to the Conquest ; for the law-loving Normans created legal fictions to meet the new
developments of the old institutions, and they
clothed the whole political life of England
with a rigid legal dress that of itself made
a new set of institutions.   But before the
Norman era, and reaching almost from the
time of the first settlement of England, the
original free communities began to be en-
croached upon by powerful aldermen and
chiefs, and manor courts gradually arose as
appendages of the power of the chief.   Then
the Normans gave them a definite position
in the political national system, by closely
knitting the feudal lords with the king and
his authority.

Under the name of manorial court, three
courts are usually included — the court
leet, the court baron, and the customary
court of the manor ; and though modern
legal theory keeps their origin apart, there

cannot be reasonable doubt that all three legitimately descended together from the primitive village council (Maine's *Vill. Com.*, 139).

They represent both legislative and judicial functions ; the court baron and customary court of the manor dealing with the proprietary rights of the community, and the court leet with the personal matters.

The duties of these manorial courts were many and significant. Every free tenant was bound to attend, and a penalty was imposed upon everyone who was absent (see *Year Book*, xxi, Ed. i, Middlesex Iter). This fine for non-attendance belongs so thoroughly to the spirit of Teutonic institutions, and is so universal, that its significance will at once be recognised.

The court baron was composed of the lord of the manor and a certain minimum number of free tenants, to sit with the lord as its judges (Ellis's *Introd. to Domesday*, i, p. 237). If there were not tenemental lands enough to supply the free tenants, it could only be upheld as a customary manorial court. Both courts are alike in their jurisdiction, though the court baron has to deal with freeholders, and the customary court with the villeins of the lord's domain.

The court baron had the right of admitting a tenant, which answers to the right of the community to determine whether a new settler should be admitted to membership ; it had the right also of determining the by-laws, the local arrangement for the common husbandry, the fencing of the hayfields (Nasse, *Agric. Com.*, pp. 17-18), the proportion of cattle to be turned into the common pasture (Nelson, *Lex Maneriorum*, pp. 59-67). It may also hold plea of any personal actions, of debt, trespass on the case, or the like, where the debt or damages do not amount to forty shillings, which is the same sum of three marks that bounded the jurisdiction of the ancient Gothic courts in their lowest instance, the fierding courts, so called because four were instituted within every superior district or hundred (*Blackstone*, edit. 1853, iii, 375.

The customary court appertains entirely to the copyholders, and in it their estates are transferred by surrender and admittance, and other matters transacted relative to their tenures only. Again we have to note that the customs of relief and surrender are remnants of the policy of the time when every transfer of property required the witness of the community, to whose membership the new tenant was thereby admitted (Stubbs' *Const. Hist. Eng.*, i, 85).

The extensive criminal jurisdiction of the court leet is amply shown by the presentment in view of frank pledge. What this actually was reflects very clearly its origin. It had to make presentment to a higher court of all wrong-doers and criminals within its jurisdiction; a presentment which very clearly replaced an actual power of its own before higher courts were instituted. The duties of this presentment as given below, are summarised by Mr. Toulmin Smith from Fleta, and other valuable authorities. To state whether the roll of inhabitants is complete; whether any have gone away

N

under any circumstances of suspicion ; whether all on the roll have come up to the folkmote ; touching burglars, thieves, and robbers, forgers, murderers, house-burners, and the accessories and harbourers of any of these ; touching outlaws and returned convicts ; touching treasure-trove, murders, and stolen goods found and kept ; touching gaol-breach, rape, abduction, and wrong-doers in parks, burrows, warrens, etc. ; touching maimings, assaults, false imprison-ments, and other breaches of the peace ; touching usurers, traitors, etc., and their harbourers ; touching petty thefts ; touch-ing the hue-and-cry wrongly raised, or, if rightly, not followed up, who raised it, and by whose default suit was not followed up ; touching land-marks broken, removed, or altered ; touching watercourses turned or obstructed ; touching ditches, walls, water-banks, pools, or anything of like sort, meddled with, damaged, or otherwise to any man's hurt ; touching ways and paths wrongfully obstructed or narrowed ; touch-ing false weights and measures ; touch-

ing watch and ward not duly kept, and
highways not well maintained ; touching
bridges and waterbanks out of repair (*The
Parish*, pp. 367-368) ; touching the adul-
teration of food (*ibid.*, 404, note ¶).

Although this seems to be a goodly
list, we have yet to add that so satisfied was
Parliament of the power of courts leet, that
even in one of those statutes on religious
matters which distinguish the latter part
of the reign of Henry VIII, it is expressly
enacted that the leets could enquire touching even heretics (*ibid.*, 615).

It would seem almost that we have exhausted the catalogue of duties belonging
also to modern vestries as well as to the
court leet ; but besides the existence of free
townships, we shall find in a later section
that parochial duties soon become distinguished from manorial rights.

Before going further, it would be useful to
give an example of the kind of duties performed in these local communities ; it will
serve to show their extensive jurisdiction,
and it will illustrate what large surrenders

local self-government has made by allowing itself to be engulfed by the centralising process which has been going on for so many years. Nowhere could we find a better example than in the Scottish baronial fiefs; and though the English manor is not quite identical with its Scottish counterpart, there is not sufficient difference in origin nor in development to vitiate the force of the example. Most important particulars of manorial documents are given in the Reports of the Historical MSS. Commission, and the following is perhaps an exceptionally valuable instance. It occurs among a large mass of documents, and consists of a—

"MSS. volume, entitled 'Court Book of the Baronies of Newtyle, Keillours, Cowty, and Bendochie', begun September 1725, when Patrick Grant, of Bonhard, Baillie, held his court at the mill of Newtyle, and at which Mr. Charles Rattray, of Gelliebanks, produced a letter of bailliary and chamberlainry, granted by Anne Countess of Bute in his favour. The courts seem ordinarily to have been held at Haltoun and Newtyle, and the proceedings illustrate the condition of agriculture in the district, and in some measure bear on points of social economy.

"In a court held on 8th November 1725, certain Acts were passed and recorded, with a direction that they should be read over once or twice in the year, when the tenants should be convened in greatest number. The Acts had the following heads :—

"1. Act anent commonties.

"2. Act anent planting and cutting of trees and breaking of enclosures.

"3. Act anent the milnes and farm meall.

"4. Act anent the moss.

"5. Act anent breaking of enclosures.

"6. Act anent vagrant persons. The tenants were prohibited from admitting any person into their grasshouses who have not a visible way of living, and are not of good fame, and bring not a sufficient testimony of their good behaviour.

"7. Act anent good neighbourhood. The tenants in use to have common herds for sheep and cattle are not to take on them to separate their flocks, or to refuse to join in the common charge of keeping herds, and that they have their respective proportions of grass, meal, and teathing of their own field, according to their proper shares, under the penalty of ten pounds toties quoties.

"8. Act anent the meadow.

"9. Act anent sward ground.

"10. Act anent smyddies.

"11. Act anent stipends.

"12. Act anent biggins.

"13. Act anent the tenants—attending courts etc.

"14. Act anent sowing of pease.

"15. Act anent complaints and assessments.

"16. Act anent the disposal of corns.

"17. Act anent millars.

"At the court which followed this one, other Acts of a like nature were passed, and bear to have been made at the instance of the Countess of Bute, 'and sanctioned by the tenants of Rose-haugh's Estate in Perth and Forfar'.

"One of the additional Acts thus enacted is against public-houses and offices not authorised, and provides 'That none presume to set up an alehouse, brew or vend ale or any other liquors, neither set up smiddies, or exercise the smith's craft, nor set up malt barns, or make malt, but by the special allowance or approbation of the master ; and when any persons are so autho-rized and appointed to exercise these different trades, that all the inhabitants of the Barony be obliged, as their occasions require, to em-ploy them ; and the brewers, smiths, and malt-men of the Barony shall be preferred to all others ; they in their respective offices giving due service, attendance, and work, to those of the Barony who employ them.   The penalty of the possessors or tenants not employing them shall be 40*s.* Scots, and the penalty of the brewers, smiths, and maltmen not doing faith-fully their parts shall be £10 Scots, besides the damages.'

"Others are 'For encouraging the enclosing

of grounds', and 'For encouraging and regulating the spinning of yarn'."[1]

From this insight into the duties of manorial courts it will have been seen what good evidence there is to show that they have descended from an archaic and complete system of polity; and it is not difficult, I venture to think, in spite of Mr. Seebohm's weighty evidence to the contrary, to prove that they owe their present form to the encroachment of modern ideas of lordship and modern political necessities, as represented by the events succeeding the English Conquest, rather than to the influences of ancient ideas and political surroundings, as represented by the influences of the Romans in Britain. This is, of course, not the place to discuss such a problem, but it will nevertheless be useful to point out one or two facts illustrative of the encroachment of feudal lords upon archaic manorial rights. Norden, writing so late as 1607, asks, "Is not every manor a little common-

[1] *Hist. MSS. Commission,* Lord Wharncliffe, v, 623.

wealth, whereof the tenants are the members, the land the bulke, and the lord the head?" (*Surveyor's Dialogue,* p. 28),—a question which is pregnant with suggestions as to the general aspect of a manor.

It has been well observed by Sir Henry Maine, that the fact of the lord himself sitting in the court baron, and having a representative of competent legal learning in the court leet, only proves that the court leet, which was entrusted with the examination of the Frank pledge, had more public importance than the other manorial courts (*Vill. Com.,* p. 140). They are, to all intents and purposes, lords' courts, or rather popular courts bearing a distinct impress of the lords' encroachment of power. The popular element, however, was not entirely eradicated by, or was not entirely separated from, the baronial elements. The free tenants had still the right to sit in the court baron as judges with the lord.

In some cases, however, the lord gained the whole of the power to himself. This is put in historical records as especial grants

of the crown. But they were the trans-
ference of rights which belonged to the
people's courts to some powerful noble or
prelate. According to English law terms,
it was the granting sac and soc. "Saca" was
the power and privilege of hearing and
determining causes and disputes, levying
forfeitures and fines within a certain precinct. "Soca" was the territory or precinct
in which the saca and other privileges were
exercised (*Laws of Ed. Conf.*, Wilkins,
p. 202, quoted by Sir H. Ellis, *Introd. to
Domes.*, i, 273). Upon this point Mr.
Pearson says:

" Having to protect and control a number
of dependants, it was natural that the noble
should attempt to withdraw them from the
operation of the local courts, in which he
had no voice. Special jurisdictions were
hence created by the side of the townships
and tithings, but with the markworthy
difference that they were not popular, but
aristocratic or feudal. Their appropriate
name was the soke, and the men subject to
them were soc-men. Their powers were

subordinate to the county gemots (*Cd. Dip.*, i, p. xlvi) ; their functions were mixed, and they have survived to the present day the shadows of ancient feudality, as courts baron for civil matters, and as courts leet for the original frank-pledge purpose, the ordering of the police, by a view of the tenantry."[1]

Dr. Stubbs, in pursuing this subject, mentions instances of special grants by the king, in which the grantee would hold the courts on his own estate (*Const. Hist.*, i, 107), and most probably in his own hall.[2]

"At the time of the Conquest", says the *Year Book of Edward I* (xx Ed. I, p. 12), "the manors with the franchises appurtenant were given to those who could lay hold of them." And bearing in mind the nature and necessities of feudal sovereignty, it will be seen how, with such grants as

---

[1] *Blackstone*, bk. iii, cap. 4, bk. iv, cap. 19 ; Pearson's *England*, p. 176.

[2] An entry in *Domesday* at Burton in Lincolnshire, indicates that an "aula", hall, or mansion, frequently accompanied the "soca".—Ellis, *Introd. to Domesday*. i, 274.

these, the lords would become more and more powerful as necessary links in the chain that bound the nation together. In places where royal grants did not directly aid them, the political requirements of the age did so ; and in places where the royal grant placed power in their hands they wielded it absolutely.

There are some interesting historical facts connected with the hall of the chief which may be noted perhaps, especially as they introduce us to a valuable series of records. The hall was a very important portion of the lord's dominion. It was the seat of justice, as well as the place of gathering upon all festive occasions, at which the chief, as in the celebrated instance of Fergus Mac Ivor, entertained his tenantry and followers. Sir Henry Ellis, in his introduction to the *Domesday Book* (i, 232), tabulates instances to show that the hall was the usual appendage of a manor, and was often used in the sense of "caput manerii", the capital village of a barony, where the baron had his principal seat and common residence. We find this hall of great importance also with the great northern peoples, whose history is closely allied with our own. Dr. Dasent, in the introduction to his *Story of Burnt Njal,* gives an elaborate description of the building, accompanied by some valuable plans showing its construction. We are not surprised, therefore, to find mention of " Halmote" records as belonging to old baronial manors. Thus in the Hatton collection, described in the first report of the Historical Manuscripts Commission, we have the *Halmote Book of the manor of Raunds* (i, 31), and the Marquis of Bath possesses a whole series of Halmote rolls, ranging from 1261 to 1540. Unfortunately, such old records as these have never yet been published, and we cannot therefore do more than be thankful to know that they exist among the rich historical archives of England.

The most important historical review of manorial customs and their archaic value is—

Seebohm (Frederic), The English Village Com-

munity Examined in its Relations to the
Manorial and Tribal Systems, and to the
Common or Open-field System of Husbandry.
London, 1883. 8vo, pp. xxi, 464.

And Mr. Elton's *Origins of English History* (London, 1883) should also be consulted. Mr. Seebohm's book has almost
revolutionised historical opinion upon the
origin of the manor. He claims for the
manorial system an origin going back to
the times of the Roman Empire, and boldly
declares that there is no evidence of the
free village community in England, but only
of a village community in serfdom under
the manor. Throughout all the pages of
Mr. Seebohm's remarkable book the student
is met by important and interesting facts
bearing upon the early social history of
the English people, and though I venture
to differ from the main conclusions he has
drawn, there can be no question that they
must enormously influence the lines of
future research.

General treatises of great value have
been published at the time when manorial

law had an extensive sway in the life of the nation ; and these books are of great importance now, for the purpose of gathering up the remnants of this old life, which has now so completely passed away.   The most important of these are the following:

The Maner of Kepynge a Courte Baron and a Lete, with diuers fourmes of entreis. playntes, processes, presentmētes, and other matters determinable there.   Newely imprynted and corrected.   Black letter, 12mo, fol. D in eights E 1. 2.   Impressum Londini in vico qui vocatur Fletstret, per me, Elizabeth Pykerynge, viduam nuper vxoram spectabilis viri Roberti Redmani.

Covrt Leete et Covrt Baron, collect. per John Kitchen de Greies Inne, vn apprentice in ley ; et les cases & matters necessairies pur seneschals de ceus courts a scier & pur les students de les measons del chauncerie ore noulement imprimee & per le author mesme corrigee onesque diuers nouel additions come court de Marshalsey ; auncient demesne. court de pipowders, essoines, imparlance, view, actions, contracts. pleadings, maintenance. & diuers auter matters.   In ædibus Thomæ Wright & Bonhomi Norton, 1598. 8vo, 11 leaves and fol. 289 ; table 3 leaves.

Crompton (R.), L'avthoritie et iurisdiction des

covrts de la Maiestie de la Roygne : neuel-
mont collect. & compose.　London, 1637.
Sm. 4to, fol. 232.

Contents : De Treshavlt court de Parliament—de Starchamber—de Chauncerie—de
Banco Regis—de hault Steward et Constable
Dengleterre—de Admiraltie de Engleterre—
de Common Banke—de Marshalsey—d'es-
cheker—de Gardes et Liueries—des Justices
de Gaole Deliuerie—des Justices de oyer et
terminer-- de Duchy de Lancaster—de counties palantine de Lancaster, Chester, et Durham et les Cinque Portes—des Justices in Eire
—des Justices del Forest—de Justices d'As-
sises et nisi prius—deschetors—de Coroners—
del Clerk del Market—de Piepowders, Faires,
et Markets—de tourne de Viscount—de Hundred et County Court.

Coke (Sir Edward), Three Law Tracts : i, The
Compleat Copyholder : being a discourse of
the antiquity and nature of manors and
copyholders. ii, ... iii, ... To which are
added the old tenures ; also some notes and
additions to Lord Coke's *Commentary upon
Littleton,* showing how the laws are altered
since those authors wrote. By William Hawkins. London, 1764. 8vo, xii, 364, the table.

Court-Keeper's (The) Companion, containing all
common business of courts leet and courts
baron : as the charges to the juries, proceedings in court and entries in the rolls ; with
precedents of copies of court-roll grants,

admittances, surrenders, presentments, etc., of copyhold estates for lives and in fee. To which is added the general customs of copyhold estates, and some special cases of law concerning them and the business of Court-keeping ; and also some necessary precedents relating to land stewardship, etc. In the Savoy: printed by Eliz. Nutt ...... 1717. 12mo, pp. 214, and table 10 pp. unnumbered.

Powell (Robert), A Treatise of the antiquity, authority, uses, and jurisdiction of the ancient Courts of Leet ; or, View of Frankpledge, and of subordination of Government derived from the institution of Moses, the first legislator, and the first immitation of him in this island of Great Britaine by King Alfred, and continued ever since: together with additions and alterations of the moderne lawes and statutes inquirable at those courts untill this present yeare 1642, with a large explication of the old oath of allegiance, and the king's royall office of protection annexed. Published by Robert Powell, of New Inne, gent. London, printed by Richard Badger, 1642. Sm. 4to, pp. A 3, 241.

Scroggs (Sir Will., Knt.) [sometime Lord Chief Justice of England, published from the Manuscripts of], The Practice of Courts Leet and Courts Baron, with full and exact directions for making up Court-Rolls, as well of Courts Leet as of Courts Baron : as also the

manner of drawing and entering all sorts of
presentments and forfeitures in courts leet,
and of surrenders, admissions, and reco-
veries in the nature of writs of entry sur
disseisin en le post at the common law.
Likewise several curious matters and notes in
law relating to presentments, distress, amer-
ciaments, fines, rescous, replevin, wastes,
estrays, by-laws, harriots, escheat, surrenders, etc., with directions for giving charges
to the jury and homage at a court leet and
a court baron. To this third edition are added
very large additions, and the late Acts of
Parliament concerning the duty of surrenders,
admittances, etc., the whole carefully corrected from the errors of the former impres-
sion. In the Savoy: printed by T. Nutt, as-
signee of Edward Sayer, Esq., for T. Walthoe,
in the Middle-Temple Cloysters ; and at his
shop in Stafford. 1774. 8vo, preface ; pp. 1-
498 ; the table.

Ritson (Joseph), Jurisdiction of Courts Leet.
London, 1809. 8vo.

The most important of the modern
treatises on manorial law are :

Watkins (Charles), Treatise on Copyholds.
Fourth edition. London, 1825. 2 vols., 8vo.

Elton (C. J.), Custom and Tenant Right. London, 1884. 8vo. [Appended to the essay are
a Minute of the Copyhold Commissioners
(April 1865), a short notice of Manorial

O

Courts, The Customs of Yetminster Prima, Old Forms of Primogeniture, Parliamentary Surveys, Westmoreland, and the principal provisions of the Copyhold Enfranchisement Bill, 1882.]

The best general collection of examples of tenures on land is :

Hazlitt (W. Carew), Tenures of Land and Customs of Manor.   Originally collected by Thomas Blount, and republished with large additions and improvements in 1784 and 1815. London, 1874. 8vo, pp. xv, 456. [Arranged alphabetically under the names of the manors.]

Special collections, relating to particular manors or districts, are :

Andrews (W.), History of the Dunmow Flitch of Bacon Custom.   London, 1877. 8vo.

Beamont (William), Warrington in 1465, as described in a contemporary rent roll of the Legh family, in the possession of Thomas Legh, Esq., of Lynn Park. Manchester, 1849. 4to.

[Beauchamp (Earl)], Excerpta e Scrinio Maneriali de Madresfield in com. Vigorn. [Privately printed] 1873. 4to, pp. iv, 46.

Case (The) of the Commoners of the Mannor of Epworth in the Isle of Axholme, in the County of Lincoln. [London, 169-.] Sheet folio.

Case (The) of the Mannor of Epworth concerned in the Bill for an Act for settling the
level of Hatfield Chase. [London, 169-.]
Sheet folio.

Charnock (R. S.), Ancient Manorial Customs,
Tenures, etc., of Essex. 1870. 8vo.

Clark (George Thomas), The Custumary of the
Manor and Soke of Rothley, in the county of
Leicester. *Archæologia*, vol. xlvii, pp. 89,
130.

Corner (George R.), Borough English as existing in the county of Sussex. *Suss. Arch.
Coll.*, vi, 164-189.

Croftes (Richard), Particulars of the Manor of
Little Saxham, in the county of Suffolk. Bury
St. Edmunds, 1788. Folio.

Duckett (Sir G.), Westmoreland : its Tenures,
General History, and Post Mortem Inquests.
*Cumberland and Westmoreland Antiq. and
Arch. Soc.*, iv, 13-15.

Dwarris (Sir Fortunatus), Local Laws, Courts,
and Customs of Derbyshire. *Journ. Arch.
Assoc.*, vii, 199-210.

Elton (Charles Isaac), The Tenures of Kent.
London, 1867. 8vo.

Figg (William), Manorial Customs of Southese-
with-Heighton, near Lewes. *Suss. Arch. Coll.*,
iii, 249-252.

—— Tenantry Customs in Sussex—The

Drinker Acres. *Suss. Arch. Coll.*, iv, 305-308.

Fitch (W. S.), A Catalogue of Suffolk Manorial Registers, Royal Grants and Deeds, Court Baron, Leet, and Rent Rolls, Surveys ..... and other documents, collected for the purpose of illustrating a history of the county. Great Yarmouth, 1843. 8vo.

Gad Whip Service rendered at Caistor Church for lands at Broughton, Lincolnshire. *Arch. Journ.*, vi, 238-248.

Hibbert (Samuel), Illustrations of the Customs of a Manor in the North of England during the 15th century. Edinburgh, 1822. 4to.

Imber (M.), The Case; or, an Abstract of the Customs of the Manor of Merdon, in the parish of Hursley, in the county of Southampton. London, 1707. 8vo.

Ingleby (Dr. C. M.), Shakespeare and the Enclosure of Common Fields at Welcombe, being a fragment of the Public Diary of Thomas Greene, Town Clerk of Stratford-upon-Avon, 1614-1617, reproduced in autotype, with letterpress transcript. Edited with introduction and notes by Dr. Ingleby. 1885. Sm. folio. Only 50 copies printed.

The diary is presented in two forms : 1, a reproduction, by the autotype process, of the whole manuscript ; 2, a literal transcript of the same, with the abbreviations expanded, an historical introduction, and explanatory notes.

Jones (William Arthur), The Customs of the Manor of Taunton Deane. *Somerset Arch. and Nat. Hist. Soc.*, xviii, 76-99.

Lawrence (P. H.), Extracts from the Court Rolls of the Manor of Wimbledon, extending from 1 Edward IV to A.D. 1864 ; selected from the original rolls. London, 1866. 8vo, pp. xii, 650.

Locke (Richard), The Customs of the Manor of Taunton and Taunton Deane, agreeable to the ancient Court Rolls and Customaries of the said Manor ; to which is added a particular of the fees taken by the Town Clerk of the Castle of Taunton. Taunton (no date). 8vo, pp. 74.

Maitland Club: Notices from the Local Records of Dysart. Glasgow, 1853. 4to, pp. x, 72.
    Presented to the President and Members of the Maitland Club by William Euing.

Peacock (Edward), Notes from the Court Rolls of the Manor of Scotter, Lincolnshire. *Archæologia*, vol. xlvi, pp. 371-388.

Robinson (Thomas), Common Law of Kent ; or, the Customs of Gavelkind. London, 1822. Third edition.

Sandys (Charles), Consuetudines Kanciæ : a history of gavelkind and other remarkable customs in the county of Kent. London, 1851. 8vo.

Savill (J. W.), History of Dunmow; comprising complete histories of the manors, etc. Dunmow, 1865. 8vo.

Scrope (G. Poulett), On the Self-Government of Small Manorial Communities as exemplified in the Manor of Castle Combe. *Wilts Arch. and Nat. Hist. Soc.*, iii, 145-163.

Shillibeer (H. B.), The Ancient Customs of the Manor of Taunton Deane, collected from the records of the manor. Presented by the jury at the Law Day Court, the 24th April, 1817, and published under their sanction ; to which are prefixed some introductory observations on copyholds in general, and remarks on those of this manor in particular, with the origin, history, and nature of courts leet and courts baron. Taunton, Tiverton, and London, 1821. 8vo, pp. vii, 29.

Somner (William), Treatise of Gavelkind [of Kent], both name and thing ; with his Life by Bp. White Kennett. London, 1726. 4to. [At the end is an appendix of such muniments, charters, etc. (in Anglo-Saxon) as are quoted in the preceding pages.]

The Free Cvstomes, Benefits, and Priviledges of the copyhold Tennents of the Mannors of Stepny and Hackny. At London, printed by William Jones, 1617. 4to.

Customs and Privileges of the Manors of

Stepney and Hackney, in the county of Middlesex. [London] in the Savoy, 1736. 12mo, pp. 128.

Stevens (Rev. Henry), The Dumb Borsholder of Chart, in the Parish of Wateringbury. *Arch. Cant.*, ii, 85-88.

Wentworth (George), Some Account of the Town and Manor of Wakefield and Sandal Castle. *Journ. Arch. Assoc.*, xx, 120-136.

Williams (Benjamin), An Account of the Officers in a Manor in Oxfordshire, with remarks upon the hide of land. *Arch.*, xxxiii, 269-278; xxxv, 475-479.

VII.—THE TOWNSHIP AND PARISH.

IN the previous section it has been pointed out that the manor and township descend from one archaic original. While the manor has taken upon itself all the old rights and privileges of the agricultural community, the township, under its ecclesiastical name of the parish, has become the administrative unit of the State machinery, and at the same time the sport of all the political theorists who have had the power and the opportunity of passing their theories into Acts of Parliament.

This state of things prevents one aspect of the township from being properly seen, namely, that in some instances, through the agency of local forces which cannot now be discovered, it has retained functions which almost universally belong to the stricter organisation of the manor. It is very important to note these early traces of the parent system living on in the township, because they must have an important bearing upon the history of the manorial system ; and, if I mistake not, they supply evidence of the existence of the free village community in England—evidence which Mr. Seebohm has failed to observe. It is clear that, with reference to the agricultural features of the township, there can be no question of a descent from an original village community in serfdom, if the manorial system is considered to be the legitimate descendant of that early organisation. In the township there is no lord at the apex of the community, and in his place is the township assembly. The agricultural rights and duties of this assembly are archaically of much interest, and I would urge upon students the necessity of collecting as much evidence as possible upon this subject. We cannot gather the full significance of such evidence until we have a long range of examples before us, and then I venture to think both the historian and the economist will have a word to say upon it. Already the subject has passed from its proper academical treatment to the wilder theories of political reformers ; and, again, on this account, I would urge the necessity of sifting and examining old historical progress before attempting to legislate upon the many features which belong to the domain of local self-government.

Some few examples of the agricultural rights and duties of the township must be given, and the following are selected from a mass of information which has taken years to collect.

The marshes and common lands of the parish of Tottenham, Middlesex, contain about 298 acres. The names of the marshes are : Lock Mead Marsh ; Clendish Hills Marsh; Mill Mead Marsh; Mitchley Marsh; Broad Mead Marsh; Wild Marsh. The names of the common fields are: Down Field; Hall Field. The common fields and marshes (except Mitchley) open on the 12th August for cows and horses only belonging to the parishioners, and close on the 5th April. Mitchley Marsh opens about the 26th

September, and shuts up at the same time as the others. The propriety of regulating the custom of turning cattle into the marshes was taken into consideration by the parishioners on the 17th July 1821. It appeared to the vestry, by reference to ancient documents, that the right of turning cattle into the marshes belonging to the parish rests with the inhabitant householders only; and it was ordered to be presented to the next court leet, requesting the interference of the proper officer of the manor to carry the intentions of the vestry into effect. The leet jury presented "that by the custom of the manors of Tottenham no person has a right to turn cattle into the marshes of the manors other than resident householders", and the Hayward was directed not to mark the cattle of any person except a resident householder of the parish of Tottenham. The inhabitants in vestry appointed a committee to inquire into the original rights and customs of the marshes, who, at a vestry held 29th March 1824, reported that ". . . . period of opening the marshes has been in many instances regulated by the vestry, but by 13 Geo. III, cap. 81, the power of regulating the same is vested in a majority of the owners and occupiers of the lammas lands; and that certain pieces of lammas lands had been mowed twice in one season, and other pieces fed previous to the time of opening—such practice cannot be suffered, and in case of a repetition of the same, that the lord of the manor be requested to prosecute the party offending." At a vestry held July 26, 1713, it was agreed "that whereas the season of the year being very wet, insomuch that several persons cannot gett their crops out of the marshes by Lammas day next as usuall, by reason thereof wee do hereby order that no cattle shall be turned into the said marshes untill fourteen days after Lammas day aforesaid. . . ."

These important examples of the vestry taking action in matters usually manorial are given in Robinson's *History of Tottenham* (vol. i, pp. 138, 139, 142), and there

are other examples given besides alienation
of Lammas lands by the vestry on 18th
December 1769, and 23rd August 1773.

According to Mr. Toulmin Smith (*The
Parish*, p. 464), permission is often given to
individuals, by the inhabitants in vestry
assembled, to enclose certain parts of the
common or waste within the parish, on
certain conditions ; and a record of the
transaction being entered on the Parish
Minute Book. "To some persons, who
have not examined into the subject of
parish history and acts," says Mr. Smith,
"this may be unknown ; and very likely
the title so derived may be one that many
a conveyancer would be puzzled to deal
with. It is probable, however, that there
is not a county in England in which the
sole title to good estates, or of part of good
estates, to the extent of many acres, has
no other root of title. It has been the custom in some parishes to keep a distinct
account of moneys received in consideration
of leave thus given by the vestry to make
these enclosures. Sometimes they are

entered under the name of 'Waste Land
Fund'; and a valuable parish stock has
often been accumulated by this means,
which may be appropriated to any purpose
the vestry pleases, and is thus of far more
substantial use than the right of common
over those pieces of ground ever was."
This is a remarkable factor in parish history, and too little attention has been paid
to it. The "Towne Book" of Yardley, or
Ardley, in Hertfordshire, contains some
valuable records as to the power of the
township to deal with agricultural or land
questions, and it will be well to quote
an instance. "At a convention of the
parishioners", held in 1707, among other
things it was ordered, "that no person or
inhabitant shall, at any time or times hereafter, keep within this Parish—*i.e.*, on the
common land in the parish—above the
number of one sheep to an acre, for every
acre of Arable Land in Tillage, which he or
they shall hold at yᵉ same time within this
Parish ; upon the paine of paying sureties
for his dealing "—26th Sept. 1574 (*ibid.*,

561)—"two pence for every sheep so kept
above y^t number, for every time they shall
graze in any of the comon ffields within the
said parish"—"that no person or inhabitant
shall at any time or times hereafter keepe
any sheepe in any Lane within this Parish
where the Fence on one side is not his owne,
upon paine of paying 2d. per sheepe for every
time y^t such sheepe shall graze there"—
"that every person or inhabitant within
this Parish shall, at the next Parish meeting, bring in a particular of how many acres
he has in Tillage within this Parish."
(Toulmin Smith's *The Parish,* p. 526.)
Among the records of the parish of Horn-
sey, in Middlesex, 17 March 1784, "it was
unanimously agreed that I. B. and M. H.
have part of the Common on Fortress
Green, Muswell Hill, on their paying after
the rate of thirty shillings per acre, at 24
years' purchase, allowing them two years'
purchase for the fencing" (*ibid.,* p. 531).

Two very remarkable instances from the
Kentish boroughs of Fordwich and Lydd
may not be inappropriately referred to

here, though strictly speaking they belong
rather to the section on municipal government ; but they serve to show that municipal and township government are parallel
developments distinct from manorial organisation. Of the thirty-one clauses of
the Custumale of the Corporation of Fordwich, the ninth prescribes the manner in
which lands may be bequeathed ; the tenth
explains "quomodo proximiores de sanguine
habebunt primam emptionem terrae"; the
fourteenth, "quomodo debent terrae et tene-
menta infancium infra ætatem custodiri";
and the nineteenth gives the mayor the
right of administering to the estates of in-
testates. (*Hist. MSS. Com.*, v, 607.) The
commoners of Lydd, in a code of twenty-
eight resolutions, agree thereby to forego
their rights of common on the Ripe, and in
lieu thereof to have a flock of sheep there
for the general use of the town. A town
shepherd was to be appointed for keeping
the stock, as follows : " Item, it is ordered
that yearly, at the feast of St. Mary Magda-
len, there shall be chosen a shepperd to keep

and look to the sheep of the towne, by the Bayliffe, Jurats, and Commons, as they may accord; which shepperd shall make account of the number yearly remaining, and or the increase and yearly decay of the same."

One very curious fact which is connected with this part of our subject is the existence of outlying parts of parishes surrounded topographically by other parishes. It will be remembered that the shires have the same interesting phenomenon. Some maps published by Stanford show the state of the country with reference to these divisions of parishes. Those parishes which are divided are shown by links which pass across the paper ; the long red line with two links at the end marks the separated portion of a parish. They exist all over the country.

It is very difficult to get a satisfactory explanation of this phenomenon. It has been suggested as an explanation, with reference to some of these places, that, inasmuch as it is found that many of those isolated spots are in the centres of forests, or in places where there were formerly forests in ancient times, the inhabitants of the lowland, or of the open land, had parts of forests given them for purposes of fuel; and that when the trees were cut down, and the place left bare in the middle of the forest, they claimed that land as part of their own parish (Select Committee on Boundaries of Parishes, etc., 1873, question 48). But these outlying parishes may now be amalgamated with the district in which they are situated, if the parties interested in the localities deem it advisable that it should be done, by Act 30 and 31 Vict., c. 106 (*ibid.*, 52). And this has actually been carried out in the instances of Woolavington, in Sussex, now divided into East Lavington and West Lavington; of East Lavant and West Lavant, near Chichester, now Lavant; of Shipton, in Gloucestershire; and of Dalton-in-Furness, in Lancashire (*ibid.*, 54-9).

Some of these detached portions arise out of a very archaic state of things, which I forbear from touching now; but some of

them are of modern origin, as may be
gathered from the evidence given before
the same Committee. Lord Kesteven (question 2522) says, that "many years ago a
very extensive fen land of 30,000 acres was
drained by steam power, and has become a
highly cultivated district. It was a common. About half of it was under an ancient Act of Parliament, called the Adven-
turers' Act, who undertook to drain it
in the time of Charles the Second ; but
which was never completed. They got
about half the land, the drainage of which
they did complete ; the other half was
commonable, and the Act of Parliament
was obtained, about the year 1812, to enclose
the commonable part. It so happens that
the parish in which I lived had common
rights over this land, although it is eight
miles distant. A part of the parishes in
my district are naturally in the Stamford
Union, but they are in the Bourne Union.
The local board has the power of annexing
them if they think fit, and if a necessity
arises it can be done. But there is literally

no chargeable poor. Half of this district was extra-parochial, and paid rates to no union whatever ; had no overseer, and no roads. When I was Member for the county of Lincoln, there were 14,000 acres of it in that condition, and I got a private Act passed to enclose, allot, and parochialise, and make it chargeable to the poor. They are now brought within the pale of civilisation, and have roads and a church." Modern as all this is, it will serve to guide the student of archaic English history towards finding a clue as to the course of the early settlement and colonisation by the Anglo-Saxons.

We will now speak of the ecclesiastical aspect of the township, for this is the oldest when we leave the archaic survivals just touched upon, and turn to the living jurisdiction of the smallest local units.

The parish still retains a substantial remnant of its old corporate life, clinging as it were round the parish church and burial-ground. Parochial overseers continue, as ever, to be the authorities mainly responsible for the due collection of rates, and the accuracy of registers on which electoral qualifications depend for their validity, while the habit of common parochial action is kept up by annual vestry meetings, and the choice of various representative officers—not to speak of less formal but not less popular conventions of parishioners at the village club or on the village green (*Local Government and Taxation*, Cobden Club, England, by Brodrick, page 30).

It is very important to bear in mind the original secular, as well as sacred, position of the parish church. So much is now being talked about the church that it is well to draw attention to its place among the local institutions of the people, and to ask some consideration to this phase of the subject. It may be worth while to restore the original secular position of the church ; but this cannot be done when the whole fabric has been torn down. Of course, this is not the place to discuss political problems, but it is the place to urge a consideration of the past before taking steps which will divorce that past from all possible movements in the future. As Mr. Toulmin Smith has so tersely and admirably said in one of his many writings on the "Church Rate Question" in 1856—

"Churchwardens are secular officers, whom every parish in England is, very properly, required to choose annually as its representatives, to act in its name and on its behalf, both internally and in the external relations of the parish to the State. They have many specific and important duties;—the greater part of which concern matters that have nothing at all to do with the church. What have to do with it are on behalf of the laity alone. They are the chief officers of the secular institution of *the parish;* which institution is itself the recognised and actual basis of the system of civil government in England. They are accountable to the parishioners, in vestry assembled, for all their acts and expenditure ; and they are, at present, in every sense, truly responsible, and the office is an honourable one, wherever Parish affairs are rightly managed. If just dissatisfaction exist, the parishioners can, at any time, remove either or all of the churchwardens, and choose fresh ones in their place."

On the question of the rate to cover the necessary expenses, Mr. Smith very ably points out that—

"Lord Chief Justice Coke says, expressly, in a celebrated case, that the inhabitants may make ordinances or bye-laws for the reparation of the *church*, OR a *highway*, OR of *any such thing* as is for the *general good of the public.'* And all the Judges of the Common Pleas, in another case, declare that the parish *church* 'is *like* to a *bridge* or a *highway*. A *distringas* shall issue against the inhabitants to make them repair it ; but neither the King's Court nor the Justices of the peace can impose a tax for it. The churchwardens cannot. None but Parliament can *impose* a tax. *But the greater part of a parish can make a by-law'* for a rate. This has always been the law in England : it is still the law. *There has never yet been an Act of Parliament imposing church rates,—except* (such is human consistency) *in the time of the Commonwealth*, when the *Church of England was down*, and the *Presbyterians* and *Independents* held the rule ; who then *enforced* church rates by Act of Parliament, without either the consent of or accountability to the parishioners. That Act happily became void when things changed again."

These quotations are very important in showing that the historical view of local institutions is much wider and more important than the narrow selfishness of political views, and I think they serve as very good evidence for urging an examination of the rights and principles of local self-government before it is handled by modern legislators.

To the historian and student of social life of the past, the parish registers, church-wardens' accounts, overseers' rating books, and other similar parish documents, are recognised as of great value; but they have been neglected most shamefully. How these documents have been destroyed there is much evidence to show, and a quotation from the *Gentleman's Magazine* for January 1862 (p. 71), will be a fair example of numerous other instances.

" The most ancient portion of the registers of the parish of Kingston-upon-Thames have lately been rescued under the following circumstances:—Some time since, a gentleman wrote to the vicar, the Rev. H. P. Measor, and also to the Archdeacon of Surrey, directing their attention to the fact that among the lots included in a sale by auction by Messrs. Puttick and Simpson, the well-known London auctioneers of literary property, was the 'Ancient Parish Register of Kingston - upon - Thames'. The churchwardens at once put themselves in communication with the auctioneers, claiming the register as parish property, and intimating that its sale would be objected to as illegal. It was then ascertained that the register had been sent to them for sale by a bookseller at Plymouth, who purchased it among other effects of the late Mr. Edward Gandy, into whose possession it must have undoubtedly passed among the books and papers of his brother, the Rev. Samuel Whitlock Gandy, M.A., Vicar of Kingston, who died in 1851. It appeared that the trustees of the British Museum had offered £10 for the register, and this sum was demanded by the Plymouth bookseller as the price of its restitution. To this the vicar and churchwardens naturally objected, and applied to the magistrates at Bow Street, who advised an amicable settlement of the affair. The vestry-clerk also endeavoured to get the register delivered up, and the price asked ultimately fell to £5. The credit, however, of the recovery belongs to Mr. J. Bell, solicitor, who, on becoming churchwarden, actively exerted himself in the matter, and received back the register on the payment of two guineas. It is now in the keeping of the Rev. H. P. Measor, who, as vicar, is the legal custodian. These records thus recovered commence in 1541 (three years after parish registers were ordered to be kept, A.D. 1538, 29th of Henry VIII), and continue till 1556. Between this and the date of the other registers in Mr. Measor's possession a hiatus occurs. These latter recommence in 1560, go on till 1653, when again there is a hiatus until 1668. From 1668 they continue till the present time."

Much has been done of late years to preserve these precious documents, and all will remember the Bill introduced by Mr. Borlase, to enable the Record Office in London to take charge of them. If the Bill had become law, all parochial registers in England and Wales, and all transcripts thereof in the custody of the bishops or other diocesan officers, would be placed under the control of the Master of the Rolls, and removed to the Record Office in London ; the time fixed for the removal of such of the registers as are dated after the 1st of January 1813 being postponed for a period of twenty years ; the time fixed for the removal of all the prior documents being as soon as conveniently may be after the passing of the Bill. Whether this is the right course or not seems open to argument ; but certainly something ought to be done to preserve parish registers from the wholesale destruction which formerly took place, and which again may occur at any time. Yorkshire was foremost in opposition to this bill, and at once estab-

lished a record society for the purpose of
printing the registers of the county. Many
petitions were presented against the Bill,
and one from Leeds may be quoted as a
good summary of the objections to trans-
ferring the registers to London.

"3. That the said registers and transcripts
are documents of great value, not merely from
an archæological point of view, but as affording
in many cases the only means of tracing the
pedigrees of families and the devolution of
estates, and it is of the highest importance to
the public generally that the said documents
should be carefully preserved in places where
they may be of easy access to those who desire
to consult them. 4. That it is of great importance to those who have occasion to obtain information from parish registers, especially to
the poorer classes of persons, that they should
be able to obtain such information personally
at such times as may be convenient to them,
without the necessity of taking a journey to
London. 5. That if the parish registers of
Yorkshire were removed to London, it would be
impossible for many persons who have occasion
to consult them to obtain the information they
require except at an unreasonable expense
occasioned by the necessity of making a journey
to London, or of obtaining the information
through agents unacquainted with the object in

view, and who, in consequence of being so unacquainted, would have to be directed in their search from time to time. 6. That the removal of the diocesan transcripts to the place where the parish registers are to be deposited would remove one safeguard which at present exists, and render it possible that the information contained in the registers might be entirely lost through the destruction by fire of the original and the transcripts at the same time. 7. That many of the present custodians of the parish registers are in the habit of assisting persons who apply to them by answering inquiries sent to them by post, and sending information acquired by them through long residence in, or intimate acquaintance with, the district, and by producing registers at times when they would not be accessible if in the custody of a public official."

On the whole question of parish registers, and all they may do for us in inquiring into the past, there are two books of importance, Mr. R. S. Burn's *History of Parish Registers*, a second edition of which appeared in 1862 (8vo), and Mr. Edmund Chester Waters' *Parish Registers in England, their History and Contents* (1883).

Turning to later engraftings on to the old township institution, for the purposes of

the relief of the poor the ecclesiastical and
civil parishes were identical.   In the greater
part of England the ecclesiastical parish
was quite large enough, and not excessive,
for the purposes of the statute of Elizabeth.
That was found to be the case in all the
southern part of England, and in the midland part, and in the eastern part also, but
it was found that that was not the case
throughout the whole of the country ; and
therefore in a later statute, 14 Chas. II, c. 12,
provision was made to meet the inconveni-
ence which was felt from the existence of
very large parishes "in the counties of
Lancashire, Cheshire, Derbyshire, Yorkshire, Northumberland, the Bishoprick of
Durham, Cumberland, and Westmoreland,
and many other counties in England and
Wales."   The object of that statute was to
reduce the civil parish to dimensions suit-
able for the administration of the relief of
the poor (*Select Committee on Boundaries
of Parishes, etc.*, 1873, questions 4 and 5).
It is perfectly clear from the records, that
the justices upon whom the duty was im-

posed must have divided large places in
the north of England very soon (*ibid.,* 19);
and so imperative was this power, that
Lord Mansfield decided, in a case where a
township had been separated from the resi-
due of a parish, and other parts of the
parish claimed to be separated also, that the
justices were bound to make a subdivision
of the rest of the parish. The result has
been, no doubt, that a large number of
parishes have been subdivided to a much
greater extent than was necessary ; but still
the justices felt themselves bound to ac-
quiesce (*ibid.,* 20). This went on until an
Act was passed to put a stop to it in 1844,
7 and 8 Vict., c. 101—but not before 5,355
townships were divided and separated from
the mother parish (question 152). And
the looseness of the wording of the Act of
Charles, although at first it was considered
only to apply to northern parishes, allowed
the interpretation that it might be applied
throughout the whole of England (*ibid.,* 30).

The statute of Charles II had enabled
parishes to be divided. The next process,

however, was that of uniting parishes ; and in the reigns of William III and Anne, some of the large towns and cities of England found that it would be desirable that they should form combinations of the parishes within their areas, so as to relieve the poor by a common arrangement and system of management. But there was no general law on the subject ; each district that deemed it advisable, made application for special legislation applicable to itself. The first locality which obtained any special legislation was the city of Bristol ; then follow Exeter, Gloucester, in 1701, Canterbury ; and a good many others followed during the whole of the next century from time to time. Up to the commencement of this century different Acts were passed for the cities and boroughs of the country, in which the system varied, and the constitution varied according to what was conceived to be the most convenient arrangement for their own locality (*ibid.*, 76-77).

Following upon this was the formation of the Gilbert Unions by 22 Geo. III, cap. 82.

This statute was introduced by Mr. Gilbert, a great philanthropist. The system was to combine a variety of parishes together by their mutual consent, and to have one workhouse in common. At the time when the Poor-Law Amendment Act came into operation, in 1834, there were between sixty and seventy Gilbert Unions (*ibid.*, 84-85).

Then came the Poor-Law Amendment Act, which gave power to the Poor-Law Commissioners to dissolve any union with the consent of two-thirds of the guardians representing that union; and the influence of the commissioners who proceeded throughout the country was such that they succeeded in pursuading rather more than fifty of the unions to dissolve voluntarily and form new unions; the remaining twelve or thirteen unions remained undissolved for the most part, except one or two who were found to be illegally constituted, and were so disposed of, until the passing of 31 and 32 Vict., c. 122, which gave the Poor-Law Commissioners power over the remaining unions (*ibid.*, 87).

Every Act of Parliament, it will be seen from this account, seems to take its own view of the country, and to cut it up in various ways, without any regard to existing divisions; and an amusing instance of this appeared in a letter in the *Times* of April 11th, 1877.

" Mr. George F. Chambers writes to us from 1, Cloisters, Temple :—' I live, when at home in the country in what may be called a well Board-ed parish. We have, for 13,000 inhabitants and 8,000 acres—1, a Local Board with twenty-four members, a clerk, and a minute book ; 2, a Board of Guardians with six members (for the parish), a clerk, and a minute book ; 3, a Burial Board, with nine members, a clerk, and a minute book ; 4, a Vestry meeting occasionally, in honour of which there is a clerk and a minute book, while a small section of the inhabitants would saddle us with (5) a School Board, with a clerk and minute book. Candidates for seats on these Boards are scarce ; a new face is quite a novelty. Thus, of the twenty-nine candidates who were nominated this year for our Local Board, Guardians, and Burial Board, no fewer than twenty-six had before been members or candidates for some one, two, or in one or more cases, for all three of the above Boards. I write to you to plead that the Government Burials Bill shall be amended to render compulsory the amalga-

mation of Burial Boards with Local Boards and
Urban Sanitary Authorities in the numerous
cases where the two at present exist side by side,
and with jurisdiction over identical areas. I
write also to plead that in his promised Poor
Law Consolidation Bill, Mr. Sclater Booth
should assimilate the present Poor Law election
machinery to that provided under the Public
Health Act, which happens to be the better of
the two, so that in the numerous cases of identical areas, one register of owners and one set
of voting papers should do for two purposes.
In my parish last week some 1,500 voting papers
were collected from door to door by a staff of
Local Board officials for the Local Board election. Two days later a different staff of officials
went all over the same ground to distribute
another 1,500 voting papers to practically the
selfsame body of voters for an election of Guardians. The money thus wasted in duplicate
machinery and printing amounted no doubt to
£20 or £30. Multiply this waste by the number of Local Boards in England acting for Poor
Law areas, and we shall arrive at a magnificent
sum total of money wasted, probably more than
£100,000 for the whole of England, there being
in England fully 600 Local Boards, the majority
of them ruling districts with boundaries conter-
minous with Poor Law parishes.' "

We now turn to the literature of the subject. The most important books, archæologi-

cally, on the parish are Seebohm's *English Village Community*, already noted, and Sir Henry Maine's *Village Communities in the East and West*, a third edition of which was published in 1876. A study of these masterful books will prepare the way for the more special works, by far the most important of which is :

Smith (J. Toulmin), The Parish : its powers and obligations at law as regards the welfare of every neighbourhood, and in relation to the State ; its officers and committees, and the responsibility of every parishioner ; with illustrations of the practical working of this institution in all secular affairs, and of some modern attempts at ecclesiastical encroachment. London, 1854. First edition, cr. 8vo, pp. xi, 611. Second edition. London, 1857. 8vo, pp. xii, 682.

Other books and papers to be consulted in the history of the. parish among local institutions are :

Innes (Cosmo), Origines Parochiales Scotiæ : The Antiquities, Ecclesiastical and Territorial, of the Parishes of Scotland. 1851. 3 vols., 4to.

Kennet (Bishop White), Parochial Antiquities. Oxford, 1818. 2 vols., 4to.

Brady (J. H.), and revised by James N. Mahon, A Popular Dictionary of Parochial Law and Taxation, and of the Duties of Parish Offi- cers ; alphabetically arranged : comprising assessed taxes, poor and church rates, high- way rates, watch and lamp, sewers and county rates, marriage, baptism, and burial, militia settlement and maintenance of the poor, juries and jury lists, churchwardens, over- seers, constables, vestry and vestry clerk, vicar, rector, etc., parish clerk, beadle, dis- tress for rent and taxes, etc., and generally all information likely to be serviceable to parochial authorities, or sought for by pa- rishioners and ratepayers. London, 1834, 8vo., pp. x, 421.

E. W., The Exact Constable, with his original and power in all cases belonging to his office; as also the office of churchwardens, overseers of the poor, surveyors of the highways, treasurers of the county stock, parish clerks, governor of fairs, and other inferior officers, as they are at this day establisht, both at the common laws and statutes of this kingdom. The sixth edition, whereto is added, The Office of a London Constable. 12mo, pp. 160. Lon- don, printed for F. B., Thomas Passenger and Thomas Sawbridge, 1682.

—— The Assize of Bread, with sundry good and needful ordinances for bakers, brewers, victuallers, butchers ; with statutes, ancient orders, customs of making and retailing, weights, etc.   London, 1671.   Small 4to.

Eden (Sir F. M.), State of the Poor ; or, History of the Labouring Classes in England from the Conquest.   London, 1797.   3 vols., 4to.

Fowle (Rev. T. W.), Decay of Self-Government in Villages. *Fortnightly Review*, 1879, vol. xxvi, pp. 127-209.

James (Walter H.), The Parochial Charities of the City of London. *Contemporary Review*, 1878, vol. xxxiii, pp. 67-80.

Kerslake (Thomas), What is a Town ? *Arch. Journ.*, xxxiv, 199-211.

North (Thomas), The Constables of Melton in the reign of Queen Elizabeth : a paper read before the Leicestershire Architectural and Archæological Society, at Melton Mowbray. Leicester, 1865.   8vo.

Ritson (J.), The Office of Constable.   Second edition.   London, 1815.   8vo.

Selden (John), History of Tithes.   London, 1618.   8vo.

Smallfield (J. S.), Assessment of the Parish of Cowden. *Arch. Cant.*, xi, 392-393.

The attempted legislation on parish registers has brought about a very useful energy in the publication of these documents, and the following books are specimens of the most important. There are many more titles than are here given, but the necessity for printing them here is obviated by the indefatigable industry of Dr. Marshall, who, in the *Genealogist* for July 1885 (vol. ii, pp. 193-202) gives a list of the printed parish registers.

Copy of a Book containing Registers of Births, Burials, and Marriages, and other records belonging to the General Baptist Church of Wisbeach, Cambridgeshire. Harrow, 1860. 8vo.

Cowper (J. Meadows), Our Parish Books and What they Tell Us ; Holy Cross, Westgate, Canterbury. Canterbury, 1884. 8vo, pp. iii, 150 [vol. i only].

Fletcher (W. G. D.), The Parish Registers of Loughborough, in the county of Leicester. London, 1873. 8vo.

Gatty (A. S.), The First Book of the Marriage, Baptismal, and Burial Registers of Ecclesfield Parish Church, Yorkshire, from 1558 to 1619; also the churchwardens' accounts from 1520 to 1546. London, 1878. 4to.

Glasscock (J. L., jun.), The Records of St.

Michael's Parish Church, Bishop Stortford. London, 1882. 8vo, pp. xii, 235.

Glover (J. Hulbert), Kingsthorpiana ; or, Researches in a Church Chest, being a calendar of old documents now existing in the church chest of Kingsthorpe, near Northampton, with a selection of the MSS. printed in full, and extracts from others. London, 1883. 8vo, pp. xi, 156.

Kerry (Rev. Charles), A 'History of the Municipal Church of St. Laurence, Reading. Reading and Derby, 1883. 8vo, pp. viii, 256.

Lower (M. A.), On some Old Parochial Documents relating to Lingfield. *Suss. Arch. Coll.*, xix, 36-52.

Margerison (S.), Registers of the Parish Church of Calverley, with a description of the church, and sketches of its history prior to 1650. Bradford, 1880. 8vo, 2 vols.

Peacock (Edward), On the Churchwardens' Accounts of the Parish of Stratton, in the County of Cornwall. *Archæologia*, vol. xlvi, pp. 195-236.

Turner (Rev. Edward), Ancient Parochial Account Book of Cowden. *Suss. Arch. Coll.*, xx, 91-119.

Walbran (J. R.), The First Register Book of Baptisms, Marriages, and Burials solemnised at the Chapel of Denton, in the parish of Gainford, in the county of Durham. Ripon, 1842. 8vo.

Wilkie (Rev. C. H.), St. Andrew's, Edburton, Sussex : Copy of Parish Register Book, 1558-1673. Brighton, 8vo, pp. 68.

Wright (T.), Churchwardens' Accounts of the Town of Ludlow in Shropshire, from 1540 to the end of the reign of Queen Elizabeth. London, 1869. 4to.

Each of the parishes or districts of London are compelled by the Metropolis Local Management Act, 1855, to make a report annually of the work accomplished by the vestry or local board during the year ; but besides statistical information, there is not much to be gained from these books. One notable exception, however, is the Vestry of St. James's, Westminster, the last report of which is a model which ought to be copied throughout the metropolis. Its full title is—

Twenty-ninth Annual Report of the Vestry of the Parish of St. James's, Westminster, in the County of Middlesex. 1885. 8vo, pp. 259. [This interesting volume, edited by the Vestry Clerk, Mr. Harry Wilkins, includes, in addition to the ordinary statistics and returns, some important historical information, and is accompanied by the ordnance map of 1869 and Blome's map, made from a survey in the time of Charles II—a comparison between the two showing great changes.]

We have now arrived at the end of our task, though without considering a not unimportant branch of local institutions, and one which has a very interesting body of literature attached to it—special jurisdictions. These are the liberties, the palatinates, the forests, fairs, and markets, the stannary jurisdictions, the Cinque Ports, the curious jurisdictions of the Isle of Man, and other similar institutions. They have no direct influence upon the immediate use to which the present publication, it is hoped, will be put, and therefore they are excluded, to await a more convenient opportunity.

We have before us now the great question of reform in local institutions. I shall not dwell upon this question here, because it has been touched upon in the several places where it is of immediate importance to draw the attention of the reader, and because, moreover, no-

and Blome's map, made from a survey in the
time of Charles II—a comparison between
the two showing great changes.]

We have now arrived at the end of our
task, though without considering a not unimportant branch of local institutions, and
one which has a very interesting body of
literature attached to it—special jurisdictions. These are the liberties, the palatinates, the forests, fairs, and markets, the
stannary jurisdictions, the Cinque Ports, the
curious jurisdictions of the Isle of Man, and
other similar institutions. They have no
direct influence upon the immediate use
to which the present publication, it is
hoped, will be put, and therefore they are
excluded, to await a more convenient opportunity.

We have before us now the great question of reform in local institutions. I
shall not dwell upon this question here,
because it has been touched upon in the
several places where it is of immediate
importance to draw the attention of
the reader, and because, moreover, no-

thing could be advanced here at any great length, beyond asking that all the old machinery and the traditional instincts for local self-government, which the previous chapters must have revealed, should not be carelessly laid aside to be replaced by the pet crotchets of individual thinkers, however eminent. The time has now undoubtedly arrived when Englishmen must look to their local institutions, and the first step in the way of true reform is to gather up all the deep lessons of the past : and if the Government, before attempting legislation, were to first examine by a competent machinery what is left of the old system, what has been swept away by forces inimical, and what has decayed through natural disease, they would obtain results satisfactory to future development. In India they are beginning to find out now that reform should be based upon the historical instincts of the people, and Mr. Tupper's *Punjab Customary Law* reveals how very important this discovery really is. With our speculative philosophy, we are too apt to ignore the teaching of traditional instincts. We do not, as of old, keep to old lines because we cannot think out for ourselves new lines, and we rush to the other extreme of believing new lines of so much more importance than the old. A reform based upon what is best in the past, and upon the largest and widest extension of thought for the future, is the safest way to progress, and I hope it is not too much to ask that the historical instincts of Englishmen should be made known and respected, just as the historical instincts of Hindus are.

INDEX.

A.

B.